The Reality of Management

The Reality of Management

Third edition

Rosemary Stewart

Butterworth-Heinemann
Linacre House, Jordan Hill, Oxford OX2 8DP
A division of Reed Educational and Professional Publishing Ltd

ℛ A member of the Reed Elsevier plc group

OXFORD   BOSTON   JOHANNESBURG
MELBOURNE   NEW DELHI   SINGAPORE

First published 1963
Revised edition 1979
Second edition 1985
Third edition 1997

British Library Cataloguing in Publication Data
Stewart, Rosemary
  The reality of management. – 3rd ed.
  1. Management
  I. Title
  658

ISBN 0 7506 3287 9

Typeset by Florencetype Ltd, Stoodleigh, Devon
Printed in Great Britain by Biddles Ltd, Guildford and King's Lynn

Contents

Introduction to the first edition

This book is addressed to all managers who wish to learn more about their jobs for the practical reason of becoming better managers, and to all students who seek to learn something of the realities of management. It also includes references, and a bibliography that should be useful to the management training officer.

The idea for this book developed during many discussions that followed my visits, as a guest lecturer, to management courses and conferences. These discussions took place with managers at all levels and from many different types of company. They showed two things: first, there are remarkably few books on management, apart from the purely anecdotal, that most managers do not find either too ponderous, or too theoretical, to be readable; secondly, that managers are interested in descriptions of social research into management practice and problems. (Social research is the study of people, both as individuals and in groups.) Therefore, I decided to try to write a book that I hoped managers would find both readable and useful. The material for it comes from two sources: from the research I have done during the last twelve years, during which time I interviewed over 1,500 managers about their work and problems; and from the works of other students of management.

The aim of *The Reality of Management* is to review what has been written about management in practice; to describe some of the results of social research in management which may be of value to the practising manager; and to do so, briefly, clearly and with a minimum use of jargon. Throughout I shall try to show the differences as well as the similarities of managers' jobs. I shall discuss the manager in his setting – which I shall call situation – working in a particular organization with its own distinctive character and problems; in an industry which differs in some ways from others; and in a particular locality and country where the way in which one manages is influenced by local and national traditions.

I should like to express my thanks to the Department of Economics, Massachusetts Institute of Technology, which, by kindly making me a guest from September 1961 to January 1962, gave me the time and the facilities to finish this book. I should also like to thank John H. Smith, lecturer in social science at the London School of Economics and Political Science, for his editorial help.

Introduction to the revised edition

Seventeen years have passed since this book was written, but I have been surprised on re-reading it to discover how little it dates. Much of the reality of management has remained the same. Inevitably some changes to the book are necessary. Figures and some of the illustrations must be brought up to date. There is new research that is worth telling managers about, even in a short book like this. The effect of social, political and economic changes upon managers requires, in places, a change of emphasis. Two major and related developments must be included. They are not new, but they affect more managers than they did in the early 1960s. One is the spread of active unionism to new groups of employees; people strike, or take other industrial action, who would not have done so when this book was first written. The other is the greater importance attached in Western Europe, including the UK, to workers' participation in decision-making within the organization.

In many ways it is harder to be a manager in the UK and in some European countries than it was in the early 1960s. The manager's right to take decisions without consulting staff is more often questioned, even challenged. Hence a different approach to managing is required than that adopted by many managers in the past: an approach that was discussed in the original version of this book, but which has become more essential. It is a change that is especially hard for older managers who are authoritarian by inclination, but many younger managers also complain of the decline in their authority. It is a situation that seems likely to persist, and hence one to which managers will have to adapt.

Many more people think of themselves as managers than when this book was written. Nursing administrators, hospital administrators, park superintendents, farmers, prison governors, headmasters, even bishops, are recognizing that they, too, are managers. To all of them this book is addressed.

It is an introduction that seeks to help them to understand and to cope better with the reality that they meet in their working lives. Students of management may also like to read a short introduction before they embark, as they must, on longer and weightier books.

Oxford Centre for Management Studies, 1979.

Introduction to the second edition

Many managers' jobs are harder in the mid-1980s than they were in the early 1960s when this book was first written or in the late 1970s when it was revised. That revision was a minor one. Since then external conditions have changed radically for most managers both in companies and in the public service. A major revision of the book was obviously necessary to describe the reality of management today, although the basics of managing remain the same.

Extensive changes are made in this edition to take account of the following: the shift in Western Europe from full employment to substantial unemployment, increasing world competition, pressures for more cost-effectiveness in public services, the greater awareness of the importance of management in all kinds of organizations, and the growing importance of managing information stemming from developments in computers and related technology. This new edition also takes account of later social research that is relevant to managers.

Any revision must also take account of the change in attitudes to the use of the male pronoun alone. This has been done here by making much greater use of the plural, managers, which in English fortunately has no gender; by the use of he and she; and where a single pronoun is better by occasionally using she rather than he.

Managers are under greater pressures than they were in the past. This makes it even more necessary for them to understand the realities of management and to become better managers. Therefore, a new last chapter has been added to review the common problems facing managers and to suggest how they can be tackled. There is an even greater emphasis in this new edition on making the book helpful to managers, as well as remaining suitable as an introductory text for managerial students. The order of Parts I and II is reversed as the new Part I is of more direct relevance to most managers than the first two chapters of Part II. Managers who read the book for their own guidance rather than as part of a course will probably find Chapters 1, 2, 3, 4, 8, 10 and 11 of most use, particularly 3 and 11.

Typing and retyping a new edition, even on a word processor, is more wearing than dealing with a new book. My most grateful thanks to Ann Bond for her good-humoured perseverance through all the changes. I am indebted, too, to my colleagues Dan Gowler and Nick Woodward for suggesting some of the changes that I ought to make, and to Joe Egerton for his energetic and resourceful work in the library and for his suggestions.

Templeton College: The Oxford Centre for Management Studies, 30 April 1985.

Introduction to the third edition

Today most books on management emphasize the new. They argue that the reality of management has changed and is changing in revolutionary ways. Is this true? Or, in what senses is it true? These questions underlie this new edition. It has been thoroughly revised and updated to take account of the changes, yet most of what I wrote in the first edition still holds true today: the basics of managing remain the same. There are major changes, but their extent is also exaggerated. We have, for example, come to believe that jobs are now far more insecure than in the past, yet a study of job tenure in Britain from 1975 to 1992 shows only a 10 per cent decline in the average (mean) job tenure over the period studied. The authors conclude:

> The data emphatically do not support the view that the dramatic changes in the labour market, technology and competition have spelt the end of 'jobs for life'.[1]

In the early 1960s, when *The Reality of Management* was first published, there were few management books, now there is a flood. What is distinctive about this book today? It is practical, aimed at helping managers, but bases this help on what we have learnt about management over the years. That is why it is also relevant to the university student. What is unique about this new edition is its long perspective on the current managerial fashions and the evidence it provides, in Chapter 3, on the utility of the panaceas for gaining greater staff commitment. It also distinguishes what is new from what is merely reinvention. The extent to which the same ideas are recycled over the years is well illustrated by Warren Bennis's honest comment about Mary Parker Follett's writings from the 1920s in relation to his own good writing on leadership:

> Just about everything written today about leadership and organization comes from Mary Parker Follett's writings and lectures. They are dispiritingly identical – or if not identical, they certainly rhyme – with the most contemporary of writings.[2]

One advantage of the long time perspective of this book, and its social research background, is that it makes one ask: 'What have we learnt from social research into management over the years that is relevant to the manager?', and to search for the new answers to that question as well as retaining those from the past that remain applicable today.

Producing this new edition has meant drawing on managers' experience, in my work with them over the years, and on research into management. I am much indebted to the helpful librarians and the excellent library at the University of Western Australia, Perth, where I was visiting for six weeks. I was very fortunate to have such a well-resourced library in the early stages of revising this book. I am also indebted to our own helpful librarians at Templeton College. I am especially grateful to Maggie Latham for her efficient work in preparing the original disk from the book, a dull and unusual job for a secretary these days. She was also very helpful in coping with the final stages of organizing the manuscript and disk.

Templeton College, University of Oxford, 23 September 1996.

Part One **The Job**

This section has four chapters. The first looks at the theoretical writing on the manager's functions; then at what research shows about how managers work in practice. The manager's job is divided into making decisions and getting the job done. Each of these is discussed in a separate chapter, with examples from research which should help the manager to make better decisions and to implement them more successfully. The last chapter summarizes research on leadership and what it can tell us about the nature of managers' jobs, and its relevance to the selection and development of managers.

1   What does the manager do?

What is the manager's job? To ask this question implies that there is **a** management job; that there are common elements in any management job, whether it is that of a works manager in a small firm in the light-engineering industry, a finance director in a medium-sized company selling toys, the human resources manager of a large insurance company, the marketing manager in a large charity, the director of social services in a local authority, a hospital manager, clinical director, headteacher or a farm manager. Is it possible to separate and define the similarities in all these jobs? The first part of this chapter summarizes the widely accepted theory of the manager's functions. The second part looks at what we know about managers' jobs in practice. Before that we need a brief look at definitions because it is not obvious what 'manager' or 'management' mean.

Definitions

Surprisingly such a common word as 'manager' is difficult to define because it is used so broadly. Hence even *The Concise Oxford Dictionary* offers four possible meanings, starting with: 'A person controlling or administering a business or part of a business'.[1]

Even such a short definition raises problems: what is meant by 'controlling or administering'? Clearer is the most continuously popular definition: 'Someone who gets things done through other people' or 'Someone who achieves results through other people'. Usually a 'manager' is responsible for staff, but it is possible to achieve results through others without having one's own staff. A product manager is an example, so is the senior head office specialist who may have a secretary but no other staff.

Management, manager and managing are often used interchangeably, so that helpful definitions can be found under any of these. Kast and Rosenzweig provide a good definition, which helps to explain why the term 'manager' may be applied to someone not in charge of staff:

> Management is mental (thinking, intuiting, feeling) work performed by people in an organizational context.[2] (Their definition is much longer but this is the most interesting part of it.)

A longer definition can give a better picture of what is involved in managing, such as that by French and Saward in the *Dictionary of Management*:

> To carry out the task of ensuring that a number of diverse activities are performed in such a way that a defined objective is achieved – *especially* the task of creating and maintaining conditions in which desired objectives are achieved by the combined efforts of a group of people (which includes the person doing the managing).[3]

'Management' is an even more elusive word to define than 'manager'. It has a number of distinctive meanings and which is intended may not be clear. Even the writer may be confused! The main distinction to be made – though *The Concise Oxford Dictionary* gives several more – is between management used to describe the process of managing and *the* management as a collective noun either for the board or for all the managers. When the latter is used it is often not clear who is included in 'the management'.

The manager's job: theory

Henri Fayol, a French businessman, writing in the early years of the twentieth century, used his experience to theorize about the manager's job. He described the functions that managers perform.[4] His five-fold classification has been used, with minor modifications, to the present day. First, managers must plan: set objectives, forecast, analyse problems, and make decisions about what should be done. The timescale for planning and the nature of the decisions will vary with the level of management. Secondly, managers organize: they determine what activities are necessary to achieve the objectives, they classify the work, divide it and assign it to groups and individuals. Thirdly, managers motivate: that is, they inspire their staff to contribute to the purposes of the organization, to be loyal to its aims and to pull their weight in achieving them. Fourthly, managers control what is done by checking performance against the plans. The interpretation of 'control' has changed over the years so that it is less top down. This is recognized by the change in the words that are used from *controlling subordinates to guiding staff* in setting mutually agreed objectives, establishing standards and the means of measurement for self-control. But practice does not always follow this modern rhetoric!

To these four functions, planning, organizing, motivating, and controlling, Fayol added a fifth, coordination. But this is too general a term to be satisfactorily isolated as an element in the manager's job. Coordination includes planning, as in the division of duties between jobs, and also communication if it is to be effective, as well as motivation and control. As Sune Carlson, a Swedish professor of business administration, pointed out in the first major study of what managers actually do: 'The concept of coordinating does not describe a particular set of operations but all operations which lead to a certain result, "unity of action".'[5]

A more modern attempt to theorize about the manager's job is that of Henry Mintzberg's.[6] Fayol's categories still provide the main theory of what managing is about, but Mintzberg's classification is useful because it provides a different way of thinking about the manager's job. His theories were based on a structured observation for a week each of five chief executives at work from which he sought to generalize about all managerial work. He distinguished between three main roles that a manager plays. First, there is the interpersonal aspects of the job. Second, there is the manager's role in receiving and disseminating information. This was Mintzberg's most distinctive contribution to thinking about the nature of managing at that time. He described the manager as the 'nerve center for information', but then he was writing before information technology became so pervasive. Third, there is the decision-making aspects of the job.

He subdivided the three roles into ten divisions but these do not apply to all jobs.

Peter Drucker in his numerous books over forty years has taken a different and more practical approach, as the title of one of the best of his books, *The Practice of Management*,[7] suggests. He has written about what the manager *ought* to be doing, rather than theorizing about the common characteristics of all managers' jobs. In that early book he added the development of people to the Fayol categories.

This is a theme that has continued in his later books. Today staff development is even more important than when Drucker first suggested it, because of the continuing shift away from unskilled jobs to those that require knowledgeable and self-motivated people. In later writings he reflected the growing concern for the social role of management in managing social impacts and social responsibilities.[8]

A distinction can be made in the manager's functions between *deciding what to do and getting it done*. The manager's job can, therefore, be broadly defined as 'deciding what should be done then getting other people to do it'. A longer definition would be concerned with how these two tasks are to be accomplished. The first task comprises setting objectives, planning (including decision-making), and setting up the formal organization. The second consists of motivation, communication, control (including measurement), and the development of people. The two tasks are separated for convenient analysis, but in practice they may often overlap. For instance, a manager who wishes to reach a decision acceptable to staff, and therefore more easily implemented, may include them in the process of decision-making. The increasing importance attached to participation may make it essential to do so.

It is not necessary to consider here which policy decisions are made by the board and which by management. Practice varies from one organization to another. It is sufficient for our discussion of the manager's job that all managers must be concerned, to some extent, with policy-making.

The manager's job: practice

The traditional account of management functions: planning, organizing, motivating, controlling and coordinating, is very broad. It is still repeated in many management textbooks, but what is its practical value? One test of this is whether it is a guide for the selection and the training of managers. To a limited extent it is. To know, for instance, that managers plan and motivate can help us to eliminate some people: 'He would never make a manager because he is too muddle-headed ever to be able to plan anything' or 'She is too retiring to be able to motivate anybody'. But the usefulness of such analysis is limited because the job of the manager is so varied. In one job it is important to be good at planning, in another it may be only a very minor part of the job. Even the ability to motivate others matters much more in some jobs than in others. Another test of the practical value of these five categories is whether they help managers to review how well they do their job. They are too broad and too abstract to be of any real use for this purpose.

Similarities in managerial work

A detailed study of what managers do in practice was first made by Sune Carlson,[9] who looked at the workload and working methods of nine Swedish managing directors. It was a detailed study of how they spent their time for four weeks. Carlson's findings have been confirmed by subsequent research in the US and the UK.[10] All studies show that the manager's day is typically fragmented: most managers have to switch their attention frequently from one person to another. The research gives a picture of a hectic day that contrasts with the theorists' calm description of a manager who plans, organizes and controls.

Much managerial work is necessarily fragmented, but a study by the author found that managers also fragment their work more than they need. This is rarely a conscious choice. Indeed, when managers keep a record of what they do, they are often shocked to discover the extent of fragmentation. Some of them then try to organize their work differently. One way they find of doing this is to attach less importance to being constantly available to other people.

Subsequent studies also confirmed Carlson's finding of the large amount of time that managers spend with other people. Most managers spend three-quarters or more of their time with others, and it is only in rather specialized and backroom jobs that the time may drop to about 50 per cent. Managers work with other people more than many of them realize – their estimates tend to be lower than a record of how they actually spend their time.[11] However, the studies have been done in Europe and the USA, and there may be cultural differences in the extent to which managers prefer writing to talking. Even within Europe there are differences: a comparison of the behaviour of British and German middle managers found that the latter spent more time alone.[12]

Carlson used the phrase 'administrative pathologies' to describe how his managing directors' actions differed from their views of what was efficient behaviour. He found that they tended to regard their outside activities, which took up to half their time, as a temporary burden, and hence not to plan their work to allow for them. He also found that these chief executives were rarely alone and undisturbed in their offices for periods of more than about ten minutes at a time.

The better our understanding of what managerial work is really like, the better we shall be able to select and train people to perform it well. We need to be able to generalize realistically about the nature of managerial work. The research that has been done can help us to do so. It has made us more aware, for example, of the political nature of many managers' jobs. Traditionally, attention has been focused upon the management of staff, but increasingly managers in many jobs have to be skilful at managing relations with people in other departments and outside the organization. Such relations often require political skill: the recognition of conflicts of interests and the ability to enlist support to further one's own job objectives. Some people may shy at the word 'political', and reject the idea that it may apply to their own jobs. Yet, as Leonard Sayles, in an illuminating book on managerial behaviour in practice, has written:

Perhaps the most important lesson the manager can learn concerns the nature of modern organizations. Most Americans and West Europeans are brought up to believe that consensus and unity are an essential ingredient for any successful political, social or economic institution. But this firm belief in oneness does not square with the facts. Companies, like all large organizations, have built-in divisions, and even in the proverbial 'long-run' they tend not to be eliminated. The manager must anticipate that more than one team will be playing in his organization and not find this immoral or upsetting.[13]

Happily, managers without political skills, or those who consider them distasteful, can still find jobs where such skills are not required. One of the great advantages of under-standing more about the differences in managerial work is that the match between the individual and the job can be improved.

Traditional accounts of management suggest that managing is an analytical, logical and ordered process. These accounts make managers feel guilty about their own often chaotic days. Research shows that managing is a much more human activity. Many managers, even senior ones, spend much of their time in a whirl of activity, switching their attention every few minutes from one person and subject to another. They rely and – given the brevity of many of their activities – have to rely upon the habits they have developed and upon their intuition. They choose, often unconsciously, from among all the things that they might do, those that catch their attention and that they enjoy doing. Studies of British and American managers show that they spent nearly all their time with other people, trying to find out what is happening, trying to persuade others to cooperate and less often trying to decide what ought to be done. In many managerial jobs they will need to know how to trade, bargain and compromise. The more senior they are, the more political will be the world in which they live. They will need to secure allies and to avoid creating enemies, or if they do, to gain enough power to make them harmless. The dangers that this picture of management poses to managers who are trying to be effective, and what they can do about it, are discussed in the last chapter. The comparative study mentioned above of

British and German middle managers showed that the picture of managers' behaviour just given fits British and American managers much better than it does the German middle managers. The latter have a more expert role, need to spend less time in persuasion because logical arguments carry more weight. There is a danger that our view of management is too coloured by the dominance of American experience and American management writings and for British readers by their own experience of managing in Britain.

Differences in managerial jobs

Traditional accounts of managing emphasize the common aspects. It is important to do so, but it is also important to understand the very wide differences that exist between managerial jobs. These are ignored in most books on management. Even the obvious ones are often ignored. It is different to manage in a small organization compared with a large one, though adaptable managers can make the transition. The job of a brewing manager in a brewery is very different from that of a management services manager in an insurance broking firm, even though the Fayol categories apply to both. There are differences between the two jobs in function, in industry and in the kind of people who work there. The firm's competitive position also affects what it is like to be a manager. Those who work in companies that are struggling in a highly competitive and rapidly changing industry have very different jobs from those who are managers in a company that has a major share of the market in a relatively slow-moving industry. Above all a rapid rate of change can transform a manager's job, as many managers have found out.

The differences between managers' jobs described so far would be commonly accepted. Research has identified others which can also be important in determining whether the job will suit particular personalities. One is the pattern of the day. The writer identified four types of pattern that characterize different jobs.[14] One of these patterns, called Project, is quite unlike the more usual fragmented day. The work permits, and requires, long periods of uninterrupted activity. Naturally, it suits some people better than the more normal disjointed day, while others are much happier being hectically busy. This is an example of a difference in the nature of managerial work that is rarely, if ever, taken into account in a job specification. Yet a manager who thrives on a hectic pattern of work will be unlikely to do well in a job that requires longish periods of concentrated work alone.

Another difference that is unlikely to be found in a job description is the extent of exposure that the jobholder must bear. In some jobs the holder who performs badly can be clearly identified: that is an exposed job. In others the individual's contribution to failures cannot be identified: the manager in that job is not exposed. In organizations today there are fewer such jobs.

Who the manager has to work with can have a major effect on what the job is like and what skills it requires. Managerial jobs differ in the types and difficulty of the contacts that have to be made. They thus make different demands upon the social skills of the jobholder.[15] A change from a job with one type of contacts to another with very different ones can make difficult and unexpected demands upon the manager: 'unexpected' because this is another characteristic of a job that is not adequately recognized. One of the most difficult transitions is from a post in charge of a single unit, like a retail chain store, or a post office, to a head office job where the 'political' skills of dealing with people in other departments are important.

No adequate selection and training can take place unless these differences between management jobs are appreciated. 'A good manager can manage anything' remains a common belief in Britain and America, although the expertise-based German manager would have very different views. However, it is a belief that is not much practised in many organizations in Britain and America. Changes between functions in the same organization may be fairly rare, though practice varies. Moves between companies after the age of forty, except at the top, are also uncommon, though it is easier in some occupations than in others. Two reasons are usually given for this immobility: one, the amount of technical knowledge required, particularly at the lower levels, and two, the need to know one's way round in the company. Learning the ropes is an essential part of a new manager's job. Most large organizations are unwilling to pay those over the age of thirty while they acquire this knowledge unless they have some needed expertise to offer. In general, therefore, management does not behave as if it believes that a good manager can manage anything.

The idea that a good manager can manage anything should be nearer to the truth for top management, where the technical content is lowest and where the tone is set by the managing director. Even there, the kinds of people who have to be managed and the types of problem that have to be resolved can be so diverse that they require different abilities and, therefore, different people. This was highlighted by Kotter, reporting on his study of fifteen general managers, who said that:

> We have found that the type of GM job, the nature of the business, and the nature of the corporation involved can all shape GM job demands in important ways that can require different kinds of GMs. For example, somewhat different types of people seem to be needed depending upon whether the job context is young or old, small or large, performs well or is in need of a 'turn-around'.[16]

Kotter deplored the 'I can do anything' syndrome. He found that the general managers that he studied had 'little conscious awareness just how specialized their skills, their knowledge, and their relationships really were'.[17]

Differences in what managers do

Kotter found that the jobs of the general managers whom he studied differed. He also found that the managers did their jobs differently, but this could have been explained by the distinctive nature of each job. However, studies by Stewart show that managers in similar jobs also differ in what they do.[18] Each manager does the job in his or her own way. This can be seen quite simply by comparing the amount of time spent with different kinds of contacts. One manager may be downward-focused, spending most time with her staff. Another may concentrate much more upon work with other departments. Yet another may be primarily outward-focused, spending a lot of time with people outside the organization.

Some managers get satisfaction out of performing on a larger stage than that of their own organization, and therefore make the most of the opportunities that public relations give them to do so. Managers in the more constrained jobs emphasize some aspects and neglect others. In the more flexible jobs two people in similar jobs can spend much of their time doing different kinds of work. All managers' jobs are sufficiently flexible to give managers some choice in what they do, yet managers are often unaware that they are exercising choice in what they do.

Managers do their jobs differently partly because they see them differently. Each manager starting in a new job will have a distinctive view of what needs doing. He or she will focus attention on particular problems and not notice others. Further, managers differ in what they enjoy doing and in what they are good at, and these factors also will influence how they spend their time.

The opportunities for choice that exist in managerial jobs need to be recognized by the individual manager and by all those concerned with the selection, appraisal and training of managers. So does the fact that few managers adequately recognize this choice, either in their own jobs or in those of their staff. The simile of finding a round peg to fit a round hole is quite inappropriate for the task of selecting a manager. There will always be more things in any managerial job than a particular jobholder has the time, ability or inclination to do. Hence one task in selection is to find the person who will make the choices that are most needed at a particular time.

Summary

'Managing' has proved difficult to define because it is used so widely. The most useful short definition for managing in an organization is that managers achieve results through other people. Longer definitions can be helpful in giving a better understanding of what managing means. 'Management' is used in two main senses: one, for the process of managing and the other, for managers collectively when it is often not clear whether it refers to all managers or just to the top management.

The first half of this chapter outlined the long-standing theory of managers' work as consisting of planning, organizing, motivating, controlling and coordinating. This theory developed by Fayol before the First World War is still accepted – with some doubts about whether coordination is a separate element or the key function – suggesting that, despite all the changes in the setting within which managers work, the basics of managing remain the same.

The only additional theory produced since then is that of Henry Mintzberg who argued that there are three main divisions in a manager's work: the interpersonal, the informational and the decision-making. This is a worthwhile contribution because it offers a different way of thinking about managers' work. It is more useful, because more universal, than his subdivision of the three into ten roles.

The second part of the chapter reviewed what is known about the manager's work in practice. The research into what managers do gives a different kind of picture of management. The reality of management is less planned, orderly, rational, or objective than the theory implies. Most managers – or at least British and American managers – spend their time in brief, fragmented activities, switching every five minutes from one person or problem to another. They talk or listen for three-quarters or more of the day. Managing is, even more than most managers realize, working with other people.

Managers' jobs vary so much that the statement that 'a good manager can manage anything' is not true. The similarities of managers' jobs have been overemphasized: the differences are many and important. We need, and with the help of research can make, some useful generalizations about managerial work, but we need to understand the differences, too. There are difference both in jobs and in what individual managers do. Managers in similar jobs can and do concentrate on different aspects of the job and so spend their time in different ways.

2   Making decisions

Decision-making in organizations is a popular subject for discussion and research. Recognizing that the wrong decision may cost thousands, sometimes even millions, of pounds top management is searching for ways of improving its score of bull's-eyes. Nor need it look for people who are keen to help by such varied methods as modelling decisions, using techniques to aid creativity and by the use of business games as a means of training in decision-taking. Decision-making has attracted a crowd of research workers from different disciplines. These look at the problems of making decisions from their own points of view and make their own contributions to our still limited knowledge of the subject. It would take too long to try to summarize here all these different and sometimes highly theoretical approaches to theories of decision-making.[1] Instead we shall discuss some of the simpler things that are now known about the process of decision-making in practice.[2]

Setting the sights

Decision-making in organizations is made simpler if management sets the boundaries within which the business is to operate. These boundaries are established by defining the objectives, which should be generally understood, whether implicitly or, preferably, explicitly. Writing them down can help to clarify them still further. One of the values of so defining objectives is that it will distinguish them from management beliefs, which may be shown to have no present purpose. Outdated beliefs tend to continue in any organization. In the armed services it used to be known as 'Generals always fight the last war', but it is just as true in business.

Management beliefs and attitudes are likely to have an important influence on the type of decision that is made and the speed with which a decision is reached and implemented. Some decisions may never be made because they are not in accord with management's beliefs and priorities. Others may not be implemented, or their implementation long delayed, because management, although it pays lip service to the importance of doing so, does not really believe in their value. An example of this, which is all too frequent, is the delay in implementing plans for developing managers.

Some companies publish broad objectives, reflecting their corporate philosophy. This is still more common in America than in Britain. Where it is done, the aim is to describe the values that should underlie management decisions. A particularly good example is given from an American company, Hewlett-Packard. It incorporates the idea of different stakeholders in the company, although that, now fashionable, term is not used. Profit is only one of the objectives and the aim is not maximum profit. An equivalent statement of objectives is a useful guide to decision-making in any kind of organization.

Hewlett-Packard is in the electronics industry. It first published its corporate objectives in 1957 and has modified them since from time to time. Those given below are taken from the booklet 'The HP Way', dated March 1989. The minor differences from those in a booklet of May 1979 are shown by italics for modifications and brackets for additions. The continuity is striking as the headings and most of the words remain the same. There is a greater elaboration of Our People and Citizenship than is common even today in most companies' statement of objectives.

Profit
To achieve sufficient profit to finance our company growth and to provide the resources we need to achieve our other corporate objectives.

Customers
To provide products and service of *the highest quality and* the greatest possible value to our customers, thereby gaining and holding their respect and loyalty.

Fields of interest
To participate in those fields of interest that build upon our technology and customer base, that offer opportunities for continuing growth, and that enable us to make a needed and profitable contribution.

(1979 – To enter new fields only when the ideas we have, together with our technical, manufacturing and marketing skills, assure that we can make a needed and profitable contribution to the field.)

Growth
To let our growth be limited only by our profits and our ability to develop and produce *innovative* (technical) products that satisfy real customer needs.

Our people
To help HP people share in the company's success which they make possible; to provide employment security based on their performance; *to ensure them a safe and pleasant work environment;* to recognize their individual achievements; and to help them gain a sense of satisfaction and accomplishment from their work.

Management
To foster initiative and creativity by allowing the individual great freedom of action in attaining well-defined objectives.

Citizenship
To honor our obligations to society by being an economic, intellectual and social asset to each nation and each community in which we operate.

The corporate objectives are described as 'guiding principles for all decision-making by HP people'. There is a separate list of HP's values, described as 'a set of deeply held beliefs that govern and guide our behavior in meeting our objectives and in dealing with each other, our customers, shareholders and others.' The values are summarized as:

We

have trust and respect for individuals

focus on a high level of achievement and contribution

conduct our business with uncompromising integrity

achieve our common objectives through team-work

encourage flexibility and innovation.

Each value is elaborated, for example, for the last one:

We create a work environment which supports the diversity of our people and their ideas. We strive for overall objectives which are clearly stated and agreed upon, and allow people flexibility in working toward goals in ways which they help determine are best for the organization. HP people should personally accept responsibility and be encouraged to upgrade their skills and capabilities through ongoing training and development. This is especially important in a technical business where the rate of progress is rapid and where people are expected to adapt to change.

Corporate objectives and values may not be formally set down or even formulated but a new employee will soon learn what objectives are being pursued and even more easily what values are being practised. The management of new organizations, especially, can usefully seek to think through together what are their objectives and values, but it can also be helpful to do so at other times, especially when there is major change. But it is only useful if top management exemplify the values in how they act.

More specific objectives will also be needed in any kind of organization. A company may set, for example, very specific objectives for the type of product to be manufactured and the markets to be aimed at, such as making high-quality shoes. Such specific product objectives are more likely to be found in small and medium-sized companies and in bigger companies in the capital goods industries. Similar decisions have to be made in other kinds of organizations about the range of products or services to be offered.

Organizations that are acquiring or merging with others, or investing in new developments, need to think through clearly the objectives of doing so. This should include asking: 'What business do we want to be in?' In a large and diverse group of companies the product market objectives may be very general, such as keeping in the consumer-goods industries, or there may even be no such limitation on the type of goods to be manufactured or services provided. A company that has no product objectives to guide its investment – usually where it has expanded by the acquisition of other firms must establish other objectives, such as a test of profitability. A common example is a particular return on capital. Hewlett-Packard describe a general objective for determining their 'fields of interest'.

Recognizing the limitations

The objectives are the boundaries that management sets on its freedom of decision. They establish the kind of things that management can do and those that are outside its objectives. There are also other limitations on the freedom to make decisions, but these are not self-imposed, although, in an indirect way, they may be the result of previous decisions. The first of these limitations is shortages of money, staff, and materials. Many business decisions will, therefore, mirror the economist's definition of 'the application of scarce means to alternative ends'. One of the advantages of large-scale organizations is that they are often less limited by shortages of money or staff. The second, and often stringent, limitation of managers' freedom of decision is that imposed by outside agencies, such as the government or trade unions. A third limitation comes from competitors' actions and a fourth from people's attitudes, which will be discussed in the next chapter on 'Getting the job done'.

The opposition of individual managers may mean that a decision is never reached, or, if it is, the project may flounder through lack of support. For instance, the support of the general sales manager for a proposed new product is probably essential to the success of the sales campaign. More general staff opposition can mean that a decision will never be successfully implemented. The nature and strength of opposition must be taken into account before a decision is reached.

Many limitations are not absolute bars to particular decisions. They may be overcome. Often more important, they may be anticipated and prevented from becoming a limitation. Organizations are not only subject to the economic, political and social environments within which they operate. They may also be able to partially shape their environment. Political lobbyists are well aware of that as are public relations staff!

Analysing decision-making

The ways in which decisions are made vary from one company to another, even from one part of an organization to another. There are differences in who is involved in reaching a decision, in the process by which this is done and in whether it is recorded. These differences are greater in companies than in the public services, where there are rules governing decision-making, but in any organization its culture and the style of the chief executive will affect the ways in which decisions are taken. In one company nearly all important decisions are made by a group of managers; in another, individual managers will often decide on their own. The difference between these two methods is greatest at the top. In one company there will be an active top management committee which takes the major decisions that are not the province of the board; in another, the managing director will take many of these decisions, possibly after consulting senior staff. The latter is more possible in small companies, or larger ones with a simple technology and a stable environment.

The formality of decision-making also varies. A policy decision may, or may not, be based on an agreed document or recorded in any form. In some companies there may never be a formal decision, but an understanding on which instructions are based. The latter, like the bare recording of a decision, may later lead to confusion about exactly what was agreed.

Before a decision is made, three things should be done. First, the reasons for taking a decision must be formulated. This can be done by defining a problem that is to be solved. At this stage it is vital to ask the right questions, otherwise the decision may be the right answer to the wrong question. Second, the nature of the problem must be analysed. Third, the alternative solutions must be examined, together with their possible consequences. The correctness of these preliminary stages will have great influence on the validity of the final decisions. In simple decisions these stages may be passed through very quickly.

How these steps should be carried out, and what effect they can have on the correctness of the final decision, may be illustrated by an examination of a question that many

companies have to consider at some time: 'Whether to produce a new product and, if so, which new product?' This,
like many major such decisions in any kind of organization,
is not a single decision. Usually there are a group of related
decisions, or one major decision that entails many subsidiary
ones. If top management is considering launching a new
product, the first step is to analyse why it wants to do so.
The analysis might show, for example, that a competitior's
new product is capturing some of the market; that the
company has surplus production capacity; or that the sales
force is underemployed at some time of the year. One or more
of these may be the reasons why management wants to
introduce a new product. The definition of the problem may
show that what is required is not a new product but, say,
a more interesting selling campaign for existing products. We
shall assume, however, that the definition of the problem
shows that a new product is required. We now pass to the
second stage, analysing the nature of the problem, which
tells us the kind of new product that is required. The analysis
indicates that the new product must meet two needs: diversification and the full utilization of a selling force that at
present sells one seasonal product. Therefore, the new
product must have a different sales peak from that of the
present one.

The first and second stages are now complete; a new
product is required to meet two needs. The next stage is the
examination of possible solutions against the background of
general company objectives. One solution may be found to
require the recruitment of new specialists; another may need
a heavy capital outlay; another may mean entering a market
that suffers from great fluctuations in demand; and yet
another may be strongly opposed by the general sales
manager, whose cooperation will be needed to launch the
new product on the market. How to decide which is likely to
be the best solution? Cooke and Slack warn against the idea
that there is an all-purpose list of criteria for evaluating
options, but they do suggest three broad classes of criteria:
feasibility, acceptability and vulnerability:

> The 'feasibility' of an option indicates the degree of difficulty
> in accepting it, and should assess the investment of time,

effort and money which it will need. The 'acceptability' of an option is how much it takes us towards our objectives. It is the return we get for choosing that option. The 'vulnerability' of an option indicates the extent to which things could go wrong if it is chosen. It is the risk we run by choosing the option.[3]

Feasibility includes the likelihood of implementation, particularly important when there may be opposition to the change. For some decisions it is important to consider whether they are in accord with the organization's culture or run counter to it.

Each solution may be found to have advantages and disadvantages. If time allows, some of these can be explored further. But even a thorough examination will usually leave uncertainties, such as reactions of competitiors or the amount and timing of likely market fluctuations of the product. Management will then have to decide which seems to be the best of the alternatives. Before it decides to go ahead on the selected solution, it will need to consider whether the possible advantages are worth the cost and the risks. A negative decision – not to do anything at present – may seem the wisest one. A close balance of advantages and disadvantages may be tipped by the thought of the effort necessary and the disruption that would be caused.

It is easy to have too analytical a view of decision-making and not to realize the realities that often face decision-makers. A decision may need to be made in a hurry and with inadequate information. Even when there is time to do the analysis described above it may be impossible to agree on what is the best solution. The decision-makers may disagree about what they want to happen or about what is likely to happen. The example given of a new product is more likely to arouse disagreements about the latter than the former. Such disagreements are easier to resolve than more fundamental ones about what is wanted. The price of disagreement is likely to be inaction or a compromise. The alternatives include agreeing to accept a majority decision or giving one person the power to decide when there is no agreement. What actually happens may depend upon any rules that exist for dealing with disagreements, or upon the relative force of different personalities to carry their own preferences. In more autocratically run organizations the chief executive will decide. But in many organizations, whether private enterprise or public service, the chief executive will, as one managing director put it: 'be able to get away a few times with taking dictatorial decisions, particularly if I prove to be right, but most of the time I have to persuade my staff that the decision is in their best interests, and preferably that the decision was originally their idea.'

Many managers say that they do not have time for careful preliminary investigations before making a decision. This can be a dangerous half-truth. Sometimes a quick decision is vital, and often it may not be possible to find out all the available facts, but speed is rarely the primary requirement. The old proverb, 'more haste less speed', is often applicable. Yet there are times when what is most needed is a decision, even if it may not be the best one.

Some managers dislike the idea of analysing decisions. In the business world where so much is uncertain, flair, they hold, is more important than logic. Many decisions must rest on a judgement of the relative importance of unknown factors. This is true, but it is still necessary to identify that there is a problem, especially where early recognition is important, to define it and to seek to reduce the uncertainties in identifying possible solutions.

The development of computing power has much improved the tools available to help decision-making. It is much easier to scan for exceptions, patterns and totals either visually or by using statistical methods. Computer-aided decision models are particularly useful for exploring the possible effects of alternative decisions. However, they need to be used with caution because different judgements about the scoring of the criteria used can affect the result.[4]

Benchmarking offers a different approach to trying to improve decision-making. This is the systematic comparison of practices and performance so as to stimulate performance improvement. Benchmarking can be done by comparisons within the organization, for example, between accident rates or defects in similar plants belonging to the same company, but it is more often thought of as a comparison with other organizations.

It is too early to tell whether benchmarking is only another short-lived management fad, popularized by management consultants, or whether it will become a long-term addition to ways of improving efficiency. It can be seen as a more scientific way of doing what has been done for a long time, that is, trying to learn from other people's practice. It is certainly popular at present as a Coopers & Lybrand/CBI study amongst the Times 1000 companies in 1994 said that 78 per cent of them used benchmarking and most thought that it was successful and would expect to do more over the next five years.[5]

The main benefits cited were:

- helps set meaningful and realistic targets
- improves productivity
- gives insight into new or different approaches
- motivates employees by showing what is achievable.

The last benefit is greater if employees have an opportunity to see for themselves. An early and vivid example of this comes from the reports of the Anglo-American Productivity Council reports in the late 1940s, where the British teams describe how different they found American practice.

The main problems in benchmarking described by the Coopers & Lybrand/CBI study were:

- gaining access to confidential information, especially from competitors
- lack of resources
- knowing whether the information is comparable.

The last problem also besets league tables, for example, listing performance by exam results says nothing about value added, as schools which do well with a difficult intake can rightly complain. A different kind of criticism has been made of benchmarking across countries – it is that the comparisons do not take account of the differences in the context within which the organizations work.

The British study found that benchmarking is most useful in customer service, sales and logistics and least useful in less tangible areas such as product development and research and development. An American group, the R&D Decision Quality Benchmarking Study, was set up in 1991 by the Strategic

Decisions Group in California. Their experience suggests that it is more complex to benchmark in R&D. The study identified 45 best decision-making practices and the authors suggest various ways by which management can seek to compare their practice against these: definitely not a quick fix but may provide a means of analysing one's own practice.[6]

The analysis of decisions is one way to try to improve their content. A quite different approach, which can be pursued at the same time, is to try to improve the quality of the original ideas. This matters more for some decisions than for others, more for many marketing decisions than for most personnel decisions. The Americans especially have worried about what they call 'creativity'. One of the techniques to encourage creativity is 'brain-storming', which, it is hoped, will produce new ideas. A group of people are asked to throw out any ideas on a particular subject or problem. These are all recorded, but not discussed at the brain-storming session, the sole purpose of which is to produce new ideas.

Research on decision-making

The traditional economist's picture of the businessman is of a rational being who, under the pressure of competition, carefully weighs the costs of one action against another and is preoccupied with marginal costs and marginal utility. Managers, even though they may consider this description of business behaviour to be too academic, will probably still stress the rational element in their decisions – although they may allow that the decisions made by others are often not as objective as they should be. Some economists, along with sociologists and psychologists, are interested in studying how decisions are made in practice,

Politics in decision-making

In many decisions, including investment ones, a number of studies show that hopes, wishes and internal politics play an important part.[7] The element of uncertainty in decision-making makes it easy for wishes to bias expected results. Cost estimates of a new project, for instance, may be too optimistic – a study of the management of large projects found that cost overruns from 40 to 200 per cent are the norm.[8] Some of these biases affecting decision-making may be unconscious; others may be consciously manipulated by managers who want a particular decision to be taken. One study even reports the following statement: 'In the final analysis, if anybody brings up an item of cost we haven't thought of, we can balance it by making another source of savings tangible.' The influence of wishes may also work retrospectively, so that the reasons given for failures may be quite different from the reality, although these reasons are widely accepted as facts. Management's wishes in decision-making may prevent an objective assessment of the value of a proposed project and, if it fails, also prevent an objective assessment – often any assessment at all – of why it failed. This points to a need for looking carefully at even generally accepted 'facts'. The current interest in learning organizations points to how managements can seek to overcome the weaknesses described above.

Managers can, and should strive to, improve the logic of their decisions. It is all too easy to define the problem wrongly or too narrowly, or to plump for the wrong solution. But good logic is not enough. A manager also needs to be alert to the political aspects of decision-making. One lesson that comes out of research is that decision-making must be seen as a political process. Political activity is likely when a decision affects the distribution of resources and the relative strength and status of different individuals and groups. The arguments that are put forward are likely to be coloured by the different interests affected by the decision.

Research also suggests that the description we gave of the stages in decision-making may, like the economist's models, bear little resemblance to actual business behaviour, rather it is a useful tool for checking the validity of one's reasons or for discovering what has gone wrong. Nearly forty years ago William J. Gore, reporting on some research in the USA, gave this picture of decision-making in practice:

> ... the traditional idea that a decision is an event stemming from a build-up of facts and is itself a choice between alternatives, very seldom happens. Even in what might be called

forced choice situations there may be no deliberate choice. In fact it seems tenable to hold that most decisions are not aggressive choices, and that by their nature they cannot be, for the crux of a decision is not the choice between alternatives but the identification of the costly invisible consequences of such a choice and fabrication of a choice which tiptoes its way through them without setting any of them off.[9]

All these years later, with the development of computer-aided decisions, his warning may be even more useful in preventing us from having a too theoretical and logical view of decision-making in practice.

Biases in using information

Apart from the biases introduced by politics, research has shown that there tend to be particular biases in the way that people commonly use information. Amongst the many biases that have been identified, the following are probably the easiest to watch out for:

- relying too much on available information, which has been well publicized
- looking for information to confirm one's ideas rather than for information that can prove them wrong
- giving too much weight to concrete information.

For help in overcoming these and other common biases Neustadt and May suggest that a simple breakdown of information into known, presumed and unclear will help in recognizing that known information can be acted upon but presumed and unclear information requires caution or further search.[10]

Decision-making in different kinds of organization

Anyone who has experience of business, public service and charities will know how different they are in many ways. Chairs in the National Health Service who come from business often exclaim how different they find the two. Do these differences affect the conditions for successful decision-making? Until recently there was no research that could help to answer that question. Now we have a first attempt to do so by Rodrigues and Hickson who compared 53 cases of decisions in five companies and three non-business organizations, two universities and a district of the National Health Service.[11] They found clear differences in the conditions conducive to success. In business 'a successful decision is most likely when sufficient information and sufficient means of implementation are to hand'. In the non-business organizations 'a successful decision is most likely when the right people participate and the people at the very top do not interfere too much'.[12] The researchers concluded that in a non-business organization it is important that the politics of decision-making are handled correctly. This is a finding that experienced managers in the National Health Service and other public organizations with multiple stakeholders know only too well!

Decision-making at different levels

This is a very neglected but potentially useful area of research. For any guidance we have to turn to a very old study by Norman Martin.[13] He looked at the differences between decisions at four different levels of management in a large American manufacturing company. He found that the decision situation differed in a number of ways between the levels. By 'decision situation' Martin meant the whole range, from the preliminary stages, through the actual decision and implementation, to verification of the correctness or incorrectness of the decision.

The main differences he discovered were in the length of the time perspective, the amount of continuity and the degree of uncertainty. Decisions at the higher levels had, as one would expect, a longer time perspective. From first inquiry to verification of the decision took less than two weeks in 97.7 per cent of the shift foreman's decision situations; 68 per cent of the department foreman's decisions situations were completed within two weeks; 54.2 per cent of the division superintendent's; and only 3.3 per cent of the works manager's. Half the works manager's decision situations lasted over a year; 4.3 per cent of the division superintendent's; 1.5 per cent of the department foreman's;

and none of the shift foreman's. This shows the striking difference in distant-time perspective between the works manager and the other three levels of management. Decisions at the higher levels tended to be discontinuous, as one would expect with a long time span. There were sometimes wide gaps between the different parts of the decision situation, partly due to the manager having delegated part of the process of carrying through a decision to his staff. At the lower levels all the stages tended to follow each other without a time interval, or with only a short one.

The decisions at the lower levels were much more clear cut. What had to be done was more easily seen, it usually had to be done quickly and there was less uncertainty about the result than at higher levels. At the higher levels the decision situation was much more indefinite; the time within which action should be taken was undefined, as it could depend upon the judgement of the total situation; what should be done was often difficult to decide because there were so many elements of uncertainty in the decision.

A major change since this research was done is in the radical restructuring of large organizations with a reduction in the number of managerial levels. This has given more responsibility to lower levels, but a large gap is likely to remain between the more uncertain, longer-term decisions of top management and the shorter, more clear-cut decisions of their juniors. The problem of coping well with the difference when promoted is likely to remain.

What has research contributed?

A discouraging feature of the research into decision-making is how little it has contributed that can help managers improve their decisions. The examples quoted can be of modest help to the manager, primarily in emphasizing that much decision-making is a political process and that there are biases in the use of information that one can seek to guard against. Unfortunately the comments by Mintzberg, Raisinghani and Theoret twenty years ago, at the end of a reported study, still reflects some of the limitations of research today:

We have, however, barely scratched the surface of organizational decision making. Little is known about the most important routines, notably diagnosis, design and bargaining. Diagnosis is probably the single most important routine, since it determines in large part, however implicitly, the subsequent course of action. Yet researchers have paid almost no attention to diagnosis, preferring instead to focus on the selection routines, which often appear to be just a trimming on the overall decision process.[14]

Training in decision-making

Differences in the nature of decisions at different management levels have important implications for recruitment, training and promotion. Before a management post is filled, the types of decision that have to be taken should be known. The personal characteristics and the training that a manager will need to cope satisfactorily with indeterminate decisions are likely to be different from those required for decisions made in a short time span about concrete situations. The pace of decisions will also impose demands. Some managers will, for example, relish the frequent and rapid decision-taking that characterize the job of editor of a daily paper. Others may find it too stressful and be more suited to the relatively leisurely pace of a monthly magazine.

The principal difficulty in training for decision-making is to give young managers experience in taking different types of decisions. One of the main arguments used in favour of considerable delegation is that it develops the ability to make decisions. Hence a flat organization, with a small number of management levels, should give more opportunity for decision-making at all levels. Some companies give their young managers experience of top-management decisions by putting them in charge of semi-autonomous units. Then they can feel that it is their business and its success or failure their responsibility. Such training is popular with those senior managers who believe strongly that managers learn by doing and, above all, by their mistakes.

A variety of methods are used in management education to try to improve the quality of decisions. There is broad education about the environment within which the organization operates. This can help managers to understand the factors that may be relevant to their decisions. Most effort in management education has been spent devising methods to help managers to analyse problems and to evaluate solutions. The case method is one way of helping managers to do so. The business game is another: it has the advantage of including time pressures and simulating real life by including an element of chance. Managers can be taught how to model decisions so as to evaluate uncertainties and to examine the effects of making different assumptions. These are all methods aimed at improving the rationality of decisions, but less commonly some management trainers seek to improve managers' sensitivity to the political aspects of decisions and their skills in handling these. All these methods, it can be argued, are divorced from reality, so that managers may behave differently from how they would in their own jobs. The risks of being wrong are less and so are the pressures from other parties to the decision. Most importantly, one does not have to live with the decision. Such training methods can be a useful supplement to what the manager can learn on the job, but the right kinds of job experience remain an irreplaceable training ground for decision-taking.

Summary

Management can improve the standard of its decision-making in a number of ways by:

1 Clearly defining the objectives of the business, thus setting the boundaries within which decisions will be made. If the objectives are well known, it will lessen the danger of outdated management beliefs having an influence on decisions. An example of published corporate objectives showed that these were much wider than the pursuit of profit, though that was a condition of achieving the others.
2 Recognizing the limitations that exist and affect its freedom of decision. These limitations stem from the political and social background, from competition and economic scarcities and from people's attitudes.

3 Analysing decision-making in stages to make certain that
it has formulated the reasons for taking a decision and
defined the problem to be solved; analysed the nature of
the problem; and examined the alternative solutions and
their possible consequences.

4 Being suspicious of the argument that there is no time for
such an analysis, while recognizing that sometimes what
is most needed is a decision, even if it may not be the
best one.

5 Being aware of the extent to which hopes, wishes and
internal politics distort the 'facts' presented and the criteria
for assessing them.

6 Being aware of the common biases in the use of information and taking steps to try to avoid them.

7 In public sector organizations with multiple stakeholders,
recognizing the importance of handling the politics of decision-making effectively. This can also matter in companies
but not as often.

The types of decision made at different levels of management are qualitatively different. The contrast in the length of
time, the discontinuity and the uncertainty of decisions at
senior levels, compared to those lower down, points to the
problems of selecting and training top managers who can
cope satisfactorily with these types of decision. Management
education can contribute to improving the analysis of problems and their possible solutions but cannot substitute for
experience in a job that needs such decisions. The best
training is responsibility for managing a small subsidiary.

3   Getting the job done

The second part of managers' jobs is getting things done through people. To do so successfully, managers must solve three different types of problem: those of organization, communication and cooperation. First they must allocate and coordinate the work efficiently. They must decide what to delegate, to whom, and how much. They must also decide how far they wish to spell out responsibilities, defining in detail what they want done. Their decision will be influenced partly by the nature of the organization, partly by their managerial philosophy and partly by their assessment of the capabilities and personalities of staff. They will need to know whether the work is done satisfactorily, hence what forms of control to use. Again they will be influenced by their own attitudes to management and by their judgement of their staff or of the contractors that they use. Some managers feel most comfortable with a close control, so that they know what is happening all the time; some may prefer to encourage their staff to check their own performance against mutually agreed standards.

Even where managers decide on their own what needs doing, they must still convey this to their staff and enlist their cooperation in doing it. Unfortunately some managers are not aware that either may cause a problem. Their attitude to implementation may be summed up as 'one gives one's subordinates an order and they carry it out'. Many difficulties come from a failure to recognize the importance of clear communication and willing cooperation. Any manager has to be concerned with both, although the forms of communication and the methods of obtaining cooperation may vary to some extent, depending upon the characteristics of both the manager and the managed. A foreman on a construction site talking to a labourer, for instance, will use a different language and a somewhat different approach from that of the managing director of a chemical firm talking to scientific colleagues.

The importance of effective communication and willing cooperation is most often underrated by those managers who still attach primary importance to their technical role, whether as engineers, chemists, accountants or nurses. Such managers may only learn slowly and painfully that people often misunderstand and may be suspicious of the manager's intentions; therefore, implementation will go more smoothly and speedily if the manager takes time to explain what is wanted and to listen to any objections. The management equivalent to 'a stitch in times saves nine' is 'an explanation at the start saves confusion and delay later on'.

Communication

Communication is successful when it is understood in the fullest sense, that is, both in verbal meaning and in intention. Managers cannot become good at it by learning a number of techniques. True, they can improve their communication by clearer thinking and better presentation: knowing what one wants to say, and saying it as simply and clearly as possible, will reduce the risks of misunderstanding. But they are certainly not the whole answer to how to get across what one means. There is even a danger that too much attention to communication, particularly to techniques, may distract attention from the need for cooperation, and without cooperation clear communication is useless.

Good techniques are not enough, because communication, if it is to be successful in getting people both to understand and to do what is wanted, is a cooperative or two-way process. Its effectiveness depends as much, if not more, on the attitude of the recipient as on the verbal skill of the manager, on the former's ability and willingness to listen as well as on the latter's clarity and sensitivity. It also depends on whether subordinates will say if they have not understood. Communication is, therefore, inseparably linked with cooperation. Communication is also a two-way process in a different sense in that managers do not merely give advice and instructions but they also receive advice and information on which to base decisions. Good upwards communication is as important as good downwards communication. Both can cause difficulties, for what managers say to their staff may be misunderstood or misinterpreted, and what they are told may be inadequate or untrue.

Difficulties in downwards communication can arise for a number of reasons. The first need for managers is to realize – and many do not do so sufficiently – that what they are saying is often misunderstood. They must, therefore, be prepared for such misunderstandings and, as far as possible, try to guard against them. The second is to be able to recognize their causes. Verbal misunderstanding, which is the simplest, may be due to a different use of language, especially likely when people have very different backgrounds; to lack of clarity; or to technical jargon. They may also arise from the general tendency to distort, quite involuntarily, any message passed on by word of mouth, which is illustrated in the children's game of repeating a story from person to person. A more difficult barrier to communication is caused by distrust, often leading to a wrong interpretation of what is said and to greater distortion if the message has to be passed on. Where there is an atmosphere of suspicion, even the simplest remark and the most straightforward instruction will be examined for hidden meanings. Managers may find to their astonishment that fantastic interpretations have been put on what they said or, worse, they may go on believing that their staff have understood.

The frequency with which management instructions are misinterpreted, and the nature of such misinterpretations, can be a good indication of the level of morale. Perhaps managers should remember, even if they do not feel like acting on it, Dostoyevsky's advice in *The Brothers Karamazov*: 'If the people around you are spiteful and callous and will not hear you, fall down before them and beg their forgiveness, for in truth you are to blame for their not wanting to hear you.' Unfortunately for the manager it may be past policies, throwing their shadow forward, which are to blame rather than anything that the present management has done.

Barriers to communication may also be created by a failure to understand that other people have different backgrounds and experience and therefore often do not see and interpret things in the same way. The more widely different the background, the greater the danger of misunderstanding. Yet even people who have similar educational and social backgrounds may make different assumptions, which, if not recognized, can lead to serious misinterpretations. This was illustrated in Tom Burns's study[1] of four men: the manager of a department and the two production engineers and chief designer reporting to him. It showed that half the time the staff thought that their manager had given them information or advice that they could take or not as they thought best, but he thought that he had given an instruction or a decision, which was, therefore, to be obeyed. This was a failure in communication that arose from different assumptions about the role of the manager and the amount of freedom that should be exercised by his staff. This study dates back to the 1950s but misunderstandings can always arise between people and especially between managers and their staff.

Misunderstandings are most likely to arise when there are differences in values which lead to different criteria for judgment. Management needs to make very clear what are its own values not merely by what it says but even more important by what it does. What is acceptable behaviour and what is not need to be made plain.

Managers need to be sensitive to the areas in which misunderstandings are likely. One of the most unusual, and perhaps one of the most neglected, is that of promotion. Many managers seem unaware of the amount of suspicion, speculation and rumour that so often surrounds promotions. Doubts and suspicions are intensified when managers are secretive about a new appointment, and then they are surprised if a new manager, whose appointment has caused much speculation and resentment, does not get full cooperation.

Misunderstanding is one risk in upwards communication, another is that managers may be given incorrect or incomplete information; further they may only be told what they have definitely asked about. In the interest of avoiding trouble, or of not worrying them, managers may receive a simplified, edited and sometimes wholly untrue version of what is happening. If they do, it will usually be their own fault. They may have made staff afraid to tell the truth, or anxious not to hurt or worry them. Or they may have asked questions, particularly about other staff, which are unlikely to be answered truthfully. Such questions should not be asked. Managers should recognize that people tend to cover up for each other, particularly if they are members of the same social group. Yet another barrier to upwards communication can be the manager's unwillingness to listen to employees' problems and hence to recognize the need for corrective action.

Problems in communications upwards and downwards are a long-running problem in management as studies at different periods show. An American survey of 11,000 hourly paid employees in thirty-seven companies between 1978 and 1981 found the greatest dissatisfaction was with communications. In general, employees had a favourable view of their supervisors but an unfavourable one of middle and upper management, because they thought corporate communication was bad. Half of those surveyed thought that both upwards and downwards communication was poor and only a third that it was good.[2] British organizations, at least, seem to be getting better at such communication as a survey of more than 1,500 employees, in April 1993 by the Department of Employment in the UK, found that the majority of employees said that the methods of upward and downward communication used in their workplace gave them information and allowed them to express their views.[3]

Managers, because they tend to underrate the difficulties of communication, usually exaggerate the extent to which it takes place. One illustration of this is the dual assumptions made by many managers that their staff know what they think of them, and also that they can come and discuss their careers and personal hopes and fears with them when they wish. Yet in practice the day-to-day communications between managers and their staff are on immediate work matters, and discussions about an individual's progress and career may rarely, if ever, happen informally.

So far we have talked about upwards and downwards communication, but much communication also takes place horizontally. It is essential that it should do so, especially when the implementation of a decision affects several departments. Those at the same level should be able to sort out the bugs as they develop and not be prevented by isolation or jealousies from doing so. Top management should, therefore, try to encourage communication between departments at all levels. It can do this partly through the formal organization by the use of interdepartmental committees and working parties. It can also try to foster informal contacts by giving managers opportunities to get to know those in other departments. This is one of the values of company management training courses. The location of departments, hence who shares the toilets and the coffee machine, also shapes informal contacts.

The appraisal and development interview is one example of a formal provision for communication which should, if it is done properly, be a two-way one. Unless these interviews are official policy, few managers will initiate such a discussion with their staff, since they may find it embarrassing. Still fewer staff will do so, even if their manager has an open-door policy. Often the first the manager knows of one of her staff's feelings about her progress is when she comes to say that she is leaving for another job.

Performance appraisals if they are well done and linked to an opportunity to discuss the individual's development can be a useful method of improving communication. A review of 113 studies of performance appraisals published between 1980 and 1990 found that performance feedback improved job satisfaction.[4]

Cooperation

An understanding of what has to be done is necessary for successful implementation; so is a willingness to do it. Implementation may fail because the manager's staff or fellow-managers do not cooperate adequately. Again, as in communication, it is helpful to be aware of the possible difficulties in enlisting cooperation. Is there likely to be opposition; if so, from whom and why? Can this opposition be overcome? Is the plan worth the time and effort that may be necessary to do so?

Wise managers know the limits of their authority and, as far as possible, avoid weakening it by trying to exercise it where it is likely to be challenged or ignored. Changes in fashion, for example, may require changes in management's ruling on what is appropriate dress. For female staff more than male staff it would be unwise for management to try to enforce a policy of what is acceptable dress that requires their staff to be unfashionable. Uniforms may be accepted but not restriction on ordinary dress.

Most of what we shall have to say concerns cooperation of workers, but the cooperation of other managers is also vital. Failure to obtain it may have more serious consequences than a failure with one's immediate staff. Staff who will not cooperate may resign or be moved, but the other managers are likely to remain. Hence 'acceptability to colleagues' often remains one of the prime criteria for management selection. Yet acceptability alone is sometimes too passive a quality to ensure successful implementation. Persistence, drive and political manipulation, supported by an understanding of other managers' motives and a correct assessment of the political situation in the organization, may all be necessary to get some plans implemented.

One of management's main worries, now and even more in the past, is how to get the workers' cooperation. A common management pitfall in trying to do so is the desire to find a single solution. Hence the search for panaceas, which for many years has been so marked a feature of management's approach to management – worker cooperation. Each new panacea is seized on enthusiastically by anxious managers. But alack for those who seek an easy solution! Experience and research show that there is no such thing. Any one of the popular answers may be of limited usefulness, given reasonably good morale, but none is the whole or even a major part of the answer and probably all can make a bad atmosphere even worse. Let us look in turn at each of these attempts to promote cooperation and see what lessons can be learnt. The history of each of the panaceas will be sketched to give a cautionary perspective to current hopes and fashions.

Enlisting staff cooperation: the panaceas

Management's wish to do so has a long history, but the need to do so has become more urgent. Competitive pressures have increased and so has the search for ways to get more for the taxpayer from the public sector. One approach to enlisting cooperation, discussed below, is to try to get greater commitment from the staff. Another response to competition, which is discussed in Chapter 5, is organizational restructuring.

Participation

The advocacy of employee involvement as a way of encouraging better management–worker relations and of increasing productivity has a particularly long history. The widespread practice of such involvement is relatively recent. The extent of employee involvement can range from the rather formalized arrangements for joint consultation via employee representatives, as in the long-standing Whitley Committee, to opportunities for more widespread discussion about ways of improving quality or productivity, as in quality circles, to participation in decision-making. A different, and for management, much simpler form of employee involvement is profit-sharing, which is discussed below.

The first official support for employee involvement in Britain came towards the end of the First World War, when the Whitley Committee, in a report approved by the government, recommended that national joint councils should be voluntarily set up in any industry sufficiently organized to make that possible. These councils should, in addition to settling wages and conditions of work, discuss the '*better utilization of the practical knowledge and experience of the workpeople*' and 'improvements of processes, machinery and organization, and appropriate questions relating to management and the examination of industrial experiments, with special reference to *cooperation in carrying new ideas into effect and full consideration of the workpeople's point of view in relation to them*' (our italics). The wording shows that this early report went far beyond the limited idea of joint consultation to include modern ideas of employee involvement. Not surprisingly, this, like some other post-war suggestions for improving management–labour relations, was too much in advance of its time to get much support.[5] Joint consultation was practised in some companies, but the main positive result of this recommendation was the establishment of such committees in government departments, named after the original Whitley Committee, which continue to this day.

The next major attempt to promote joint consultation came from the urgent need in the Second World War for maximum munitions production. Joint Production Consultative and Advisory Committees were set up in many munitions industries. In the words of the engineering agreement, 'The functions of the Committee' were 'to consult and advise on matters relating to productivity and increased efficiency for this purpose, in order that maximum output may be obtained from the factory'. Some of these committees continued after the war. The post-war nationalization Acts provided another boost to the establishment of joint consultative committees. These instructed the Boards to join with the unions to provide the discussion of matters affecting the safety, health and welfare of persons employed . . . and of other matters of mutual interest . . . including efficiency. . . .' Each nationalized industry therefore established its own system of consultative committees from local to national level.

During the post-war economic crisis the government again turned to the advocacy of joint consultation as a means of improving productivity. This time the idea was much more enthusiastically received by private industry than it had been after the First World War. Lectures and pamphlets, which may be taken as an index to the amount of interest in a subject, poured forth in the immediate post-war years, extolling and explaining joint consultation.

Interest in employee involvement as a way of improving productivity and quality has grown with increasing competitive pressure. A survey by the Department of Employment in 1993 found that 85 per cent of employees said that their employers used at least one form of employee involvement – similar findings came from surveys of employers.[6]

Participating in decision-making is a more active form of participation and one that means management ceding some of their decision-making power unlike joint consultation, suggestion schemes or profit-sharing which are also included in surveys of employee involvement. Hence studies of employees' views on this are a better guide to changes in management's approach to enlisting commitment. A recent study, by Kessler and Undy, of British workers, which covered a representative sample of over 1000 private and public sector employees, asked whether there was a programme at their place of work to get them more involved in decision-making.[7] Only 27 per cent said that such a programme had been introduced; 44 per cent would have liked such a programme. Overall 19 per cent were very satisfied with the influence they had in company decisions over their job or work life; 49 per cent were somewhat satisfied; 20 per cent not too satisfied and 10 per cent not satisfied at all. Employees in large organizations and trade unionists tended to be less satisfied.

Kessler and Undy also looked at the areas where the workers wanted to have an influence on decision-making and whether they felt that they had. Most important for them was to be able to influence how they did their job and organized their work: 44 per cent thought that they had a lot of influence and 25 per cent some influence. This type of influence is probably the major change that has taken place in British industry: partly, at least, it reflects the change to more team-working and the creation of self-directing work groups in some companies. The second most important area for the workers surveyed to have an influence was over the setting of health and safety standards and here only 9 per cent said that they had a lot of influence and 17 per cent some influence. Setting goals for their work group or department was also seen as very important by 37 per cent, somewhat important by 38 per cent, but only 8 per cent thought that they had a lot of influence here and 17 per cent some influence.

Participation in decision-making makes more demands on management than the other forms of employee involvement. Many European countries have gone further than the UK where such participation is rare. It seems likely that British managers will have increasingly to learn to live with such participation, and those with European subsidiaries and plants are already having to do so. How successfully they manage to do this will depend upon the level of trust created.

Despite the support often voiced for workers' participation in decision-making, research provides no clear evidence that it results in higher productivity than management decisions without participation. This was the conclusion of an article by Locke, Schweiger and Latham, which reviewed the evidence from a large number of studies. It all depends: participation in decision-making may improve productivity, it may not and can even have a bad effect. Research is only beginning to show under what conditions it will be effective. A key require-ment, the authors suggest, is that the subordinate can bring expertise to the decision-making.[8]

Profit-sharing

The supporters of profit-sharing have had even higher hopes of its value than the advocates of joint consultation and participation. (The two are not, of course, mutually exclusive; both may be practised in the same firm.) The most important among the declared objectives of management, according to a 1950 review of profit-sharing by the International Labour Organization,[9] were:

1 The prevention of strikes and the improvement of the morale of the workers.
2 The provision of an effective incentive to greater efficiency and increased output.
3 The achievement of a measure of flexibility in the total payroll enabling an automatic adjustment of the total remuneration of labour to business fluctuations.
4 The reduction of labour turnover and stabilization of the labour force.
5 The promotion of thrift and a sense of security among the workers.
6 Greater publicity for the firm.
7 The preservation of capitalism by giving the worker a stake in its continued existence.

It is noteworthy that this list is a hard-headed managerial benefits one, which contains, with the possible exception of 7, no reference to the management philosophy behind it.

In spite of this formidable list of advantages, there has been a high death rate amongst profit-sharing schemes from that date to the present day.

The ILO review of profit-sharing in 1950 concluded that:

The history of profit-sharing in all countries where it has been left to the voluntary enterprise, as in the United Kingdom and the United States, is full of examples of plans started with high hopes and ended in failure, sometimes after many years of operation.

In a few, rather exceptional cases it has been a spectacular success, but judging from the long list of abandoned plans and the comparatively small number that have endured for more than a few years, the contribution that profit-sharing can make to the promotion of healthy and happy industrial relations and to more efficient production seems to be rather problematical.[10]

The earliest known schemes date back to at least 1820 in France, 1860 in England and 1869 in the USA. Interest in profit-sharing and co-ownership schemes has continued, stimulated by employees' increasing demands for greater participation in industry. More positive government encouragement was provided in the UK as a result of the recommendations of the 1978 Finance Act for a clearer tax benefit when a company uses part of its profits to acquire shares for employees through a trust.[11]

A 1978 survey by the British Institute of Management of 622 companies in the UK found that 40 per cent of them had some kind of profit-sharing scheme, but of those 246 companies 71 per cent distributed cash, not equity shares. Less than one-quarter of the cash-distributing companies said they would consider handing out shares even if a tax advantage was gained.[12] By 1984, after some changes to the share option scheme in the 1981 Finance Act, there were 7000 schemes with 1.5 million people covered.[13] A 1990 survey of employers' practices in Leicester and Reading found that about a third had profit-sharing schemes and about a fifth had employee share schemes. They were seen primarily as ways of attracting, motivating and retaining employees rather than as a direct way of improving productivity.[14]

Quality circles

Quality circles are a much more recent panacea, although they are a form of participation.[15] They have an appeal because they are an introduction from Japan, and British, and even more American, managers have been keen to try to discover the reasons for the success of Japanese management. Quality circles are the way of giving effect to the Japanese support for bottom-up management. They consist of small groups of between five and ten employees who work together and volunteer to meet regularly to solve job-related problems. The circles are usually but not always led by the supervisor and generally meet in company time, weekly or monthly. They aim to improve quality, reduce production costs, raise productivity and improve safety. Participants decide their own topics for discussion. All are trained to use techniques of quality management, including elementary statistics.

Three assumptions underlie quality circles: one, that all employees are capable of improving efficiency and quality; two, that there is a reservoir of relevant knowledge among employees which is not easily tapped by other methods; and three, that quality is an integral part of production and is the responsibility of every employee. The method is distinctive but the idea of the reservoir of relevant knowledge underlying quality circles echoes the statement by the Whitley Committee during the First World War quoted earlier.

The quality circle movement has spread round the world. In Japan, where it started, 4 million employees were estimated to be in circles in 1978. In 1981 there were reported to be circles in 750 US corporations and governmental agencies and in more than 100 British companies. There were also circles in many other countries.

A study by Bradley and Hill, in the early 1980s, of the experience of quality circles in five US and five UK companies, and a more in-depth study of the experience in one British and one American manufacturing company, points to the potential value of quality circles and to their limitations in a different cultural setting.[16] In the two companies, quality circles had produced efficiency gains. The authors say:

> Our investigations support the evidence available in published sources, that harnessing employees' accumulated job knowledge shows through in the bottom line, and demonstrates, in addition, that employees themselves believe they have a significant contribution to make.

The authors also found that the circles improved communication between labour and management, but they point to difficulties:

> Line managers suggest by their actions that they do not fully trust quality circles, and attempt to guide the harnessing of employee expertise lest it expose managerial inadequacy or organizational ineffectiveness. The fact that some quality circles

in these two companies and elsewhere have already withered confirms that successful institutionalization can be difficult to achieve in Western companies.

Quality circles like the other methods discussed are not a panacea for improving management–worker relations. They are one possible method, amongst others, of trying to reduce the level of distrust between labour and management.
As the authors conclude:

> If they are going to be effective and have a long-term future, then the most senior levels of management must be actively involved and demonstrate a continuing commitment to provide the conditions necessary for their success.

A conclusion that is equally true for other initiatives with similar aims.

A Canadian company, CAE Electronics, has been experimenting with quality circles since the late 1970s. A report in 1995 said that they had found that the keys to success in quality circles are: 1. Involve everyone from the beginning; 2. Use facilitation; 3. Be flexible; 4. Communicate success; 5. Start slowly and build on successes; 6. Be patient.[17]

The interest in quality circles expanded in Britain in the first half of the 1980s, but then decreased. Even at its peak it has never been a common method of trying to involve staff: only 2 per cent of all enterprises and 5 per cent in manufacturing firms.[18]

Total Quality Management (TQM)

An aspect of the more recent panaceas is their emphasis on improving quality. In part this reflects the growth of service industries and in part more knowledgeable and demanding customers. Japanese focus on quality is yet another reason why companies in the West have had to take it more seriously than before.

TQM is a more highly organized, more systematized, approach to trying to enlist staff's interest in improving quality by feeding information back to them as well as a set of statistical techniques for analysing variance. Like the other panaceas it has met difficulties and for similar reasons. An article in *Fortune* in 1993 said that surveys show that two out of three managers in organizations trying TQM believe it has failed.[19] It gives five rules for success: 1. The CEO has to be involved; 2. Customer focus is critical; 3. TQM should be linked to a few clear strategic goals; 4. Demand a financial payback; 5. In a reasonable time period.

The 'be patient' advice about quality circles quoted above applies even more because TQM is wider ranging. Two American writers, Troy and Schein, argue that it takes eight to ten years to implement TQM fully within a company.[20]

More radical advice is given by Grant, Shani and Krishnan:

> TQM is a challenge to conventional management techniques and to the theories that underlie them. Therefore it cannot simply be grafted onto existing management structures and systems. If its benefits are to be fully realized, then companies need to prepare themselves for organizationwide change – including top management's relinquishing of power.[21]

They advise that the first stage in managing a TQM programme is to recognize its revolutionary character. A few American companies, they say, including Xerox, Ford and Hewlett-Packard have been successful in doing this, but many have not.

Many others have not tried. A 1995 article reporting the US Census Bureau's National Employer Survey found that only 37 per cent of the nearly 3,000 plants and offices surveyed had adopted TQM. There was an even smaller take-up of some of the other well-publicized new approaches: 25 per cent used benchmarking and 13 per cent of non-management workers participate in self-directed teams.[22]

The interest in TQM in Britain is more recent than in the US and there has been little research to tell us about experience here, but there seems no reason to believe that the findings of the American research are not applicable in the UK.

Incentive payment systems

The advocates of participation in all its forms believe that it will stimulate and encourage the workers to take more interest in the company, to identify with it and therefore to wish to increase productivity. A different approach, although, again, not a mutually exclusive one, is the belief that workers will produce more if doing so increases their earnings: hence payment by results, which was for many years, and is still often today, the most popular method for enlisting workers' cooperation in high productivity. One of the more recent changes has been the extension of incentive payment systems to professional, technical, administrative and managerial groups.

Incentive schemes have a long history, and they come in many enthusiastically advocated and vigorously decried types and forms. The literature on the subject is immense, but much of it is too partisan to be of use in trying to find out whether and, if so, in what circumstances and in what form, an incentive payment system can be of help. However, there is also a considerable amount of research results.

R. Marriott first reviewed the research and opinion on the subject in 1957 and published his fourth edition in 1971. He goes on to say that:

> Social scientists are agreed that however potentially effective a financial incentive may be, it cannot reach its maximum of effectiveness, and, in fact, will often fail unless installed and maintained in the most encouraging circumstances.[23]

One of the Income Data Services studies[24] provides a useful guide to some of these circumstances, as follows:

> The scheme must be individually tailored to suit the organization involved.
> The role and purpose of the scheme for all the participants must be spelt out.
> The conditions peculiar to the organization involved, internal and external, will dictate the most appropriate scheme. Failure to recognize these conditions has caused many of the problems in existing schemes. Financial gains alone should not be used to measure the success of a scheme because many intangible benefits cannot be measured in this manner.

Devising and maintaining a good incentive scheme is not easy because there are so many aspects to be considered.

Samuel Eilon lists ten golden rules, including 'facilitating others to achieve their goals should also be rewarded',[25] but even ten does not exhaust all the relevant considerations.

Monetary rewards are the most talked about incentive, but there are many others. Eilon distinguishes four other types of incentives: *monetary equivalents*, such as medical insurance and low-interest loans; *deferred rewards* such as pensions, stock options and promotion prospects; *non-monetary rewards* such as job title – upgrading titles when money is short is a well-known ploy – peer recognition and a spacious office; and lastly *negative incentives* such as a reprimand.[26]

Today, incentive schemes are much less often thought of as providing, by themselves, the necessary motivation for workers to reach an optimum level of productivity. Progressive managers now look on them, like the other panaceas, as a possible part of a much wider setting that must include human relations and technical and organizational efficiency.

This setting is all the more important since an incentive can only be effective if it increases workers' willingness to work, as distinct from their capacity to do so, which may be increased through better equipment and organization, or through an improvement in physical or mental health. All schemes for increasing employees' productivity and the quality of the work are based on the assumption – for which there is plenty of evidence – that there may be a gap, sometimes a large gap, between employees' willingness to work and their capacity to do so. This gap is not, of course, confined to manual workers, as disincentives to effort can, and do, operate at all levels of an organization. Research into motivation has sought to explain this gap and what can be done to reduce it.

Motivation

Motivation is a prime task for many managers. Many find it a perplexing one. The best way for a social scientist to become rich is to peddle an answer, particularly a simple answer, to how to motivate employees to work well for the organization. Unfortunately, research has shown that there are no simple answers. Motivation is much more complex and varied than the early theories suggested. Later research provides, according to David Guest in a review of research into motivation, little or no support for the previously popular theories of Maslow and Herzberg.[27] But there is evidence from the studies over the years that is useful to managers. First, managers need to examine their views about human nature.

The incentives that management provides for its employees will depend, at least to some extent, on its view of why people work and what they want from their work. Douglas McGregor,[28] an American social scientist, produced his famous distinction between managers who believe in Theory X and those who believe in Theory Y. The former believe that the willingness to work is mainly influenced by external factors, such as an incentive payment scheme, that people are naturally lazy and have to be motivated, pushed and prodded to work. The latter think that the desire to work is primarily internal, that most people want to do a good day's work but need a favourable environment in which to do it. If management thinks the former is more important, it will seek ways of devising effective incentives and means of checking that people are working hard. If it believes more in the latter, it will be more concerned with trying to provide a satisfactory working environment in which people are not frustrated and can take an interest in their work. Whichever it believes, most managements now probably accept the fact that staff attitudes have an effect on productivity, hence the interest in attitude surveys.

Since a large part of the manager's job is getting things done through people, it is essential to try to understand people's motivation. Managers tend to err in one of two directions in their expectations of how their staff will behave. They may expect them to react in the same way as they themselves would, and think them bloody-minded if they do not; conversely, they may think of their staff as being different human beings, with markedly different and much simpler motivations, from themselves. Most managers are aware that what they earn, though important, is only one of the things that matters to them. A useful general guide is that their staff will think the same; another is to recognize that people differ in what they consider important in a job.

A major study by Blackburn and Mann[29] of 1,000 workers
in jobs requiring relatively low skills provides, even many
years later, useful information about what these workers
wanted from their work. The authors found a wide variety of
orientations to work. The phrase 'orientations to work' is used
by sociologists to mean a persisting tendency to seek certain
goals and rewards from work that exists independently of the
nature of the work or its content. Blackburn and Mann found
that these workers' orientations included outdoor or indoor
work, autonomy, working conditions, worthwhileness, work-
mates, pay, hours and promotion. Some individuals had two
main orientations, generally one stronger and one weaker.

One of the most useful findings for the manager from
studies of people's motivations is that individuals want different things from work. They will therefore be satisfied in
different jobs and in different organizational cultures – the
culture of an organization is shown in the distinctive ways
in which employees think and act towards each other, to
their customers or clients, and in their attitudes to the organization. Management's task is to try to match what the
employee wants from work and what the organization has to
offer. This approach to trying to improve organizational
productivity will attach great importance to appropriate selection as well as to understanding the nature of the jobs in
the organization and its culture. A related approach,
discussed in Chapter 4, is to attach importance to training
and development of managers so that they suit what the
organization needs. Yet another approach to improving organizational productivity, which has been very popular in recent
years, is to change the organization. This will be discussed
in Chapter 5.

Management's task is now often seen to be obtaining
commitment from the staff. This idea underlies a bestseller
of the early 1980s, *In Search of Excellence* by Peters and
Waterman, which in 1996 is still the basis for seminars in
different countries by Tom Peters.[30] It was expressed tersely
by John Harvey-Jones, when chief executive of ICI, Britain's
largest chemical company: 'The real purpose of management
is motivation of the group to use its energy to achieve objectives.' The same idea was described more fully by McGregor,
writing more than twenty years earlier:

To create conditions which will generate active and willing collaboration among all members of the organization – conditions which will lead people to *want* to direct efforts towards the objectives of the enterprise ... *people often expend more energy in attempting to defeat management's objectives than they would in achieving them.* The important question is not how to get people to expend energy, but how to get them to expend it in one direction rather than another. For management, the answer lies in creating such conditions that efforts directed towards the objective of the enterprise yield genuine satisfaction of important human needs.[31]

Many years later William Ouchi produced his Theory Z in his attempts to see what useful lessons could be learnt for American business from the Japanese approach to management.[32] He identified their strategies as long-term employment, a specific stated organizational philosophy for each organization commonly emphasizing cooperation and teamwork, and intensive socialization. The last means that, as in the armed services, great attempts are made to teach the new recruits the ways and attitudes of the organization that they have joined. The motivational techniques that Ouchi advised as Theory Z are open communication, consultative decision-making and concern for the employee.

A useful guide for managers trying to improve motivation comes from what is called 'expectancy theory', which argues that employees perform well when they see a link between effort, performance and rewards, and that an incentive payment scheme may not be seen in this way. David Guest summarized what this theory tells managers that they should do to get a highly motivated workforce. They should:

Systematically identify goals and values within the workforce and survey attitudes and perceptions.

Provide rewards on an individual basis, tied to performance, rather than on a general basis. An overall pay rise, for example, will have little motivational impact.

Make the selective provision of rewards public, so that all employees can see a link between good performance and higher rewards. This will influence expectations.

Make sure staff have the knowledge, skills and understanding necessary to their role to translate motivation into high performance.[33]

Another potentially useful theory is 'goal-setting'; which suggests that motivation will be higher when individuals have clear and demanding goals to which they are committed and on which they get regular feedback about their progress.

The current state of research into motivation suggests that if managers want to raise motivation so that it leads to high performance, they need to consider many aspects of their personnel policy. The starting point is to recognize that the task is to obtain commitment rather than to exercise control. Next to accept that individuals want different things from work and hence will be motivated by different rewards, using the word 'reward' broadly to include the wide range of non-financial ones. This means that selection should try to match what the job offers with what the individual wants. Managers should seek to understand how employees explain what happens and whether they feel that they can control their rewards. Good communication is, therefore, vital. The more that employees see that they can influence rewards, and the rewards that matter to them personally, the more they are likely to be motivated.

No panaceas, but a challenge to management

Our brief survey of the search for panaceas to solve all problems of involving employees in improving productivity and quality shows that there are none. The belief, for instance, that payment by results is the answer to enlisting employees' cooperation in higher productivity is based on too simple a view of human motivation. Now that so many studies have shown that employees are interested in other things as well as money, that they may place a higher value on social satisfactions – that is, recognition of them as people, and congenial working relationships – than on take-home pay, there is a challenge to management. The challenge is to provide the conditions in which people will want to work and, therefore, to cooperate.

One reason why these panaceas failed to fulfil what was expected of them is that they were so often pursued without the management philosophy that would give them a chance of contributing to better relations. Both participation and profit-sharing imply a particular management–worker relation, stemming from a philosophy of management. Without the right philosophy any scheme for improving management–worker relations is hollow; with it, any scheme can be correctly seen as a possibly useful means for expressing and implementing it, rather than as a cure-all for bad relations. This philosophy must be based on a belief in the dignity and value of each individual in the company – individuals, not hands or numbers. Such a belief will carry with it a recognition that people should be consulted before changes that directly affect them are made. It should also include an appreciation that those with direct operational experience of what can go wrong can often contribute to ways of putting it right.

One problem that worries some top managers is how to make certain that their junior and middle managers have the same philosophy as themselves. This is particularly likely to be a problem when there is a change in top management, for instance, through privatization, or a merger. A new, more progressive top management may find that the middle managers, especially, have quite different ideas of the way employees should be treated. This can be one of the reasons why there are so many management changes when a new top management comes in.

Since the philosophy of management is vital to the relations between management and its employees, what kind of people are made managers is one of the most important decisions for an organization. To this problem we shall, therefore, turn in the next chapter.

Summary

A manager who is to be successful in getting decisions implemented by other people must organize efficiently, communicate clearly, and secure people's willing cooperation. One danger is that many managers underrate the difficulties of communication, both of conveying to their staff what they want done and why, or of getting reliable information from them. Hence, they may be startled when their actions and motives are misinterpreted. Another danger is that managers may fail to realize the need to enlist the cooperation of staff. Yet another is that, although aware of the need, they may expect some panacea to be the answer to the problems of winning cooperation.

We looked at the history of participation, profit-sharing, incentives, quality circles and TQM and saw that there is no evidence that any of them are the talisman that so many managers are looking for. At best they may be a useful tool where management–staff relations are already good. So many attempts to improve employee cooperation fail because they are based on the wrong assumptions about motivation and derive from the wrong management philosophy. Research into motivation shows that managers should consider many aspects of their personnel policy if they want to improve motivation. The problems of securing willing cooperation pose a challenge to management: a challenge to provide the conditions in which people will want to work, and, therefore, to cooperate. The prime task is to obtain commitment rather than to exercise control.

4 Leadership and development

'Leadership' sounds more dynamic than 'management': it has an emotional appeal. The British and Americans are particularly keen on the word – the Americans even more than the British. Hence it is often used in these two countries instead of management, with 'leader' instead of 'manager'. Yet leading is only one aspect of management, an aspect that is more important in some jobs, and at some times, than others. Sometimes it is vital for success, sometimes it is unnecessary. It is more important in times of difficulty and of rapid change than in stable and routine settings. It is important when the manager needs to enlist commitment to a difficult or dangerous task, hence the interest in leadership in the armed services. It is vital when a change of direction is needed and people must change their attitudes and customary ways of working. This was true for many organizations in the 1980s and remained true in the 1990s, hence the call for leaders. What 'leaders' meant was managers who had the ability to point the way and to get people committed to going that way. This ability matters most at the top of the organization, particularly of one that needs to change rapidly.

The great outpouring of books on leadership in the last ten years reflects the felt need – particularly in the USA – for leaders who can show the way forward in these times of rapid change. Some are excellent reads and some may help the manager, either as inspiration or, less often, for their practical advice.[1]

There are many definitions of leadership, as is true of any much studied subject. Common to most of them is the capacity to influence others. The *Collins Concise Dictionary* defines leader as 'a person who controls, guides or inspires others'.[2] Other even simpler definitions are 'to guide' or 'to show the way'. Academics have produced many more elaborate ones that seek to explain what is behind leadership.

The nature of leadership and what makes for effective leadership have been major subjects for research in the USA since the late 1940s. So great has been the volume of research that a large handbook summarizing the results was first published in 1974 and a third revised version in 1990.[3]

Much of the research, though called leadership studies, is equally applicable to understanding management. It is merely that the word 'leader' has been preferred to 'manager'. There are, of course, studies, particularly of leadership in small groups, where the word leader is the correct one. The first part of this chapter presents the research findings that are relevant to managers.

Research into leadership

Leadership qualities

What are the characteristics of a good leader or a good manager? This question has remained popular over many years. Multitudinous qualities have been said to be not merely desirable but essential for a good manager. The usual lists of vague, undefined qualities are no help in management selection and development. They also call for paragons, whereas all organizations must make do with imperfect human beings. However, there have been attempts to make more carefully defined lists. Two of the lists given below were compiled many years ago. They are included because they remain thought-provoking. A third more modern list is added, but since it is more technical, deriving in part from personality tests, it may be of less interest to some readers.

The first list is of the characteristics of successful businessmen compiled by Professors Edwards and Townsend in 1965, who said that 'in varying combinations and proportions these qualities seem to be found in the leadership of most businesses that have grown substantially':[4]

1 'Strength and willingness to work hard, immensely hard in some cases.
2 Perseverance and determination amounting at times to fanatical single-mindedness.

3 A taste and flair for commerce, an understanding of the marketplace.
4 Audacity – a willingness to take risks that are sometimes large gambles.
5 Ability to inspire enthusiasm in those whose cooperation and assistance are essential.
6 Toughness amounting in some men to ruthlessness.

The second list was compiled by Professor Argyris in 1953.[5] It is limited to characteristics that he thought were helpful in becoming and remaining a successful executive operating in competitive conditions. The characteristics were drawn from observing numerous American executives, so would not all be possessed by any one executive. This is in contrast to the previous list, which was of qualities likely to be found in most successful businessmen. Argyris's list is:

1 Exhibit a high tolerance of frustration.
2 Encourage full participation and are able to permit people to discuss and pull apart their decisions without feeling that their personal worth is threatened.
3 Continually question themselves, but without being constantly critical of themselves.

These executives, we would like to emphasize, were keenly aware that their personal biases, their personal ways of seeing the world, were not necessarily the only or the best ways. . . . They respected their own judgement, not as always being correct, but as always being made with the best possible intentions. Their self-respect seemed to enable them to respect others.

4 Understand the 'laws of competitive warfare' and do not feel threatened by them.
5 Express hostility tactfully.
6 Accept victory with controlled emotions.
7 Are never shattered by defeat.
8 Understand the necessity for limits and for 'unfavourable decisions'.
9 Identify themselves with groups, thereby gaining a sense of security and stability.
10 Set goals realistically.

That list is over forty years old but remains relevant today, though no. 9 may be less applicable now.

These two lists portray widely different personalities. In part this is because the first list was compiled by economists and the second by a psychologist. It is noteworthy what very different qualities they select as being important: so much so, that it is likely that even if they had been looking at the same people they would still have emphasized different qualities as the reasons for success. The difference between them highlights the key role company recruiters may play in determining the kinds of personalities who are selected. The use of search consultants and assessment centres should reduce that effect today.

The contrast between the two lists is also due to a difference in the kind of successful executive who is being analysed. The first list seems to be limited to the heads of companies, the second lists seems to include managers at different levels. (Neither of the authors are very specific on this point.) The former deals with the entrepreneur, the latter the professional manager. Both lists could be useful, in different circumstances, in the examination of promotion potential, but it would be essential to know what kind of top manager was needed. Fortunately the best predictor of success is not the possession of a long list of qualities, but prior success in similar roles. Hence evidence of leadership at school and university is a good predictor of future leadership ability, but that depends upon the situation being compatible with the individual's personality.

Argyris's list can be compared with a more modern analysis of the characteristics of successful British chief executives by Cox and Cooper in 1988[6] based on interviews and personality tests:

- determination
- learning from adversity
- seizing chances when presented
- achievement orientation and a very positive attitude to life
- internal locus of control . . . clear 'internal reference-points', which were used to guide action
- well-integrated value system
- effective management of risk

- clear objectives
- high dedication to the job
- intrinsic motivation
- well-organized life
- pragmatic approach
- sound analytic and problem-solving skills
- high level of 'people skills'
- high level of innovation
- type A personality ... which comprises a very aggressive, high-achieving, competitive and hard-driving lifestyle.

Bernard Bass, in his third edition of the massive Bass and Stogdill's *Handbook of Leadership*, summarizes the findings of research over the years into leadership characteristics as follows:

> The leader is characterized by a strong drive for responsibility and for completion of tasks, vigor and persistence in the pursuit of goals, venturesomeness and originality in problem solving, drive to exercise initiative in social situations, self-confidence and a sense of personal identity, willingness to accept the consequences of his or her decisions and actions, readiness to absorb interpersonal stress, willingness to tolerate frustration and delay, ability to influence other people's behavior, and the capacity to structure social interaction systems to the purpose at hand.[7]

This summary, and comparisons with the three lists above, suggests that the characteristics of effective leaders in Britain and the USA have remained similar over the years. It is leadership style that has to adapt to the people and the situation.

Are there some things that all good leaders do? This is one of the questions that interested research workers on leadership. A ten-year inter-disciplinary programme at Ohio State University in the 1950s studied the behaviour of leaders in business, education, the armed services and government. The researchers decided that trying to define the qualities of a good leader was unsatisfactory, and sought instead to define leadership in terms of performance. After a lot of work they finally reduced the basic functions of a good leader to two:

1 *Consideration or human relations*, that is, 'the extent to which the executive, while carrying out his leadership functions, is considerate of the staff'.
2 *Initiating structure or 'get the work out'*, that is, 'the executive organizes and defines the relationship between himself and the members of his staff. He tends to define the role which he expects each member of the staff to assume and endeavours to establish well-defined patterns of organization, channels of communication, and ways of getting jobs done.[8]

The original research was of bomber pilots[9] but the same characteristics exist in industry and in other organizations. Indeed, these two key tasks form the basis for much subsequent research into leadership. They are also still used in training programmes. Good managers should be above average in developing warm relations with their staff and in initiating new ways to solve problems, but the relative importance of the two will vary in different types of work.

There is a conflict between human relations and getting the work out, a conflict known to many managers. Staff demand that their managers should be both powerful and popular, that they should both initiate ideas and move their group towards the goal on the one hand and be considerate on the other. The conflict may be resolved by sharing the roles between two leaders, so that one leader is powerful – gets things done – and the other is popular and looks after the social and emotional needs of the members. One often sees this sharing of leadership qualities, particularly at the top of an organization. It is helpful for managers to be aware of the existence of this conflict and, therefore, of the nature of the choice before them. Managers who are unaware of this conflict may fluctuate in their attempts to satisfy first one demand and then the other, whereas what matters is that both demands are being satisfied within the group, not that the manager must be equally good at both.

The emphasis on this split in the leadership role comes from the USA where the account of the long-standing training programme, the Blake and Mouton managerial grid, has had its thirtieth year reprint.[10] The grid formulation is also available in some twenty-five languages. In the managerial grid, managers are rated from 1 to 9 on a high concern for production and 1 to 9 on a high concern for people. The ideal style is 9,9 where operating requirements permit: 'It is leadership attitude, which should be consistent, not the specific details of its implementation.'[11] Blake in 1994 (Mouton is dead) reviewing the effects of trends and practices of management argues that the trend is towards 9,9 as a dominant style because of the changes in relationships within organizations. He also argues that this is true across different cultures, nationalities and religions and sees the more autocratic 9,1 style found in some developing countries evolving towards 9,9.[12]

This is likely to be an optimistic view. Even in developed countries the evolution is likely to be slow. A survey of the views of over 1,500 European top and middle managers on their chief executives by Management Centre Europe in 1988 found a big gap between their ideal and the reality and they concluded:

> Analysing the results of their staffs' perceptions, too many of today's leaders are tough, solo-fliers, who have never heard of participative management or team building.[13]

The 9,9 manager is still likely to be an ideal rather than a reality. Perhaps it need not even be the ideal as despite the grid's use for training over many years its validity has been seriously questioned.[14] Also there is evidence from German (see Chapter 8) and Japanese managers that a greater emphasis on the task can work well. A study by White and Trevor of Japanese companies in Britain found that the British workers accepted the task-oriented approach of the Japanese managers, perhaps because it was accompanied by a more egalitarian approach.[15]

One of the questions asked by the research workers on leadership is: 'What are the effects of different methods of leadership?' Much of the early research tried to compare the effects of a democratic leader – that is, one who encourages participation – with those of an authoritarian leader. Most of it pointed towards the desirability of the democratic type of leader who encourages participation, places employee welfare before production, but does not give the former undue emphasis, and exercises only a general rather than a close supervision. However, a supervisor can be too employee-centred and this may lead to low production and low morale. Democratic leadership encourages long-term employee development and commitment. Not all employees like a democratic manager; those who have authoritarian personalities prefer an authoritarian boss. Worst of all is *laissez-faire* leadership, which has a bad effect on productivity, cohesiveness and satisfaction.

Leadership, in terms of the ability to influence others, is not necessarily identical with formal status. We all know that the amount of influence that a person exerts is a combination of position and personality. Hence it is not surprising that a key finding of the leadership studies is that leadership in a group may not be concentrated in one person but spread among several. This is illustrated by the previously mentioned two people between them meeting the needs for consideration and for getting the work out. Groups may have other needs, too, if they are to work effectively. Some need a person who comes up with new ideas, who can challenge the sloppy and conforming thinking of other members of the group; observers of group discussions may notice that contribution. Meredith Belbin has identified an even wider range of tasks that need to be performed in a team and his ideas are now familiar to many British managers.[16]

Different types of leader

One of the most important finds of the research is that there is not *one* leader's job. This puts the question 'What are the qualities of a good manager?' in a new perspective, since research shows that different situations require different leadership qualities and, therefore, different types of leaders and different kinds of managers. Hence, there is no one type of good manager, nor one set of qualities a good manager will possess. This will be borne out by anyone with wide experience of industry who has noticed the great diversity of character among successful managers. This finding should prompt the managers who are trying to fill a management vacancy to ask: 'What is the nature of this particular job?', 'What are its distinctive problems?' and, therefore, 'What kind of manager is needed to fill it?' Unfortunately the answer to these questions cannot be precise because so little is known about which characteristics of a job are important.

Those responsible for selecting a new manager need to consider not merely the individual's strengths and weaknesses but also those of their future colleagues. This raises most problems when a new managing director is being appointed. Does top management need a thorough shake-up? Unless it does, will the existing people be able to adjust to the new manager's leadership pattern? If not, will their resignations or difficulties hurt the company? The tendency of newly appointed leaders to replace some of their staff may be explained by the need to find people who complement them. Managers should also know their own weaknesses and seek to make up for them in the selection of their staff. In this sense there may be some truth in the dictum that 'a good manager can manage anything', because managers who know their own deficiencies in knowledge and personality can try to build up a team to complement them.

Managers who are trying to devise what is the best way for them to manage will find that there is no single answer. Useful advice is given in 'How to Choose a Leadership Pattern' by Robert Tannenbaum and Warren Schmidt.[17] They suggest that there are three factors managers should take into account: their own characteristics, those of their staff, and those of the situation.

Managers' characteristics that are important in deciding how to manage are:

1 Their value system, including their views on whether individuals should have a say in decisions affecting them; the important they attach to efficiency; the personal growth of their staff and company profits.
2 Their confidence in their staff.
3 Their own leadership inclinations, whether they are more comfortable being a member of a team or being highly directive.
4 Their feelings of security in an uncertain situation, hence their ability to delegate without feeling too worried about the resulting uncertainty of the outcome. 'This "tolerance for ambiguity" is being viewed increasingly by psychologists

as a key variable in a person's manner of dealing with problems.'

The characteristics of the staff that are important are:

1 The strength of their need for independence.
2 Their readiness to assume responsibility for decision-making.
3 Their tolerance for ambiguity; some staff have a preference for clear-cut directives, others prefer more freedom.
4 Their interest in the problem and their views on its importance.
5 Their degree of understanding of, and identification with, the goals of the organization.
6 Their knowledge and experience.
7 Whether they have learned to expect a share in decision-making.

The amount of freedom that managers can allow their staff will depend upon the extent to which there is a positive answer to the above points.

The characteristics of the situation that are important are:

1 The type of organization, including: the kind of behaviour that is customary, and the limitations placed on employee participation by the size of the establishment, the geographical distribution and the degree of organizational security that is necessary.
2 Group effectiveness; this is important when the delegation is to the group, rather than to an individual.
3 The nature of the problem: for instance, if managers have most of the information that is relevant, it may be easier for them to think it through rather than to brief one or more of their staff.
4 The amount of time available to make a decision will affect the extent to which managers feel they can involve their staff in decision-making.

Tannenbaum and Schmidt conclude that successful leaders are those who are both keenly aware of the factors that are relevant to their behaviour at a particular time, and who are also able to act appropriately. They are both perceptive and flexible. This means that when the situation calls for it they will be strong leaders and in different circumstances they will be permissive ones.

Developing managers

Millions of words have been written about how to develop managers, and fat fees are charged for attempting to do so. But what do we really know about it? One reflection of how little we know is that there is such a variety of approaches to developing managers within the same country and between countries. Despite the expansion of management education there are still those who believe that good managers are born and that little or nothing needs to, or can, be done to help their development, since this will be a natural process of a potentially good manager learning by experience and example. Managers who believe this are obviously not concerned with the problems of how to develop their staff. But the number who hold this comforting belief is steadily decreasing. The others are often worried men or women conscious of the increased demand made on management by the rapid changes affecting many organizations. They look round anxiously for those who have the potential to meet these demands. Once found, how are they to be given the necessary training and experience?

Increasingly the main answer in some countries has been to rely on business schools to do the bulk of management education. This answer has been most popular in the USA, where in 1990, about 75,000 MBAs graduated, one-quarter of all the masters degrees awarded that year.[18] It has been a less popular answer in Europe, though in some countries the numbers have been increasingly rapidly, partly because many young professionals and managers see that in times of such uncertainty they must manage their own careers and judge that an MBA will improve their career prospects. MBAs have developed and are increasing in many other countries. For example, India awarded about 7,000 MBAs in 1994.[19] Helping to establish and teaching on overseas MBAs provides export earnings for American business schools, particularly in Latin America, Australian schools in Singapore and Malaysia and European schools in China.

But what kind of MBA? There is the traditional academic MBA which started in the USA and is still popular there. The focus is on acquiring knowledge. It suits the academically inclined and those looking for analytical work in staff posts or as consultants. The second type of MBA, which is becoming popular in Britain, combines experience, using projects in organizations, and knowledge. It can more easily than the first be done while continuing to work and suits the more practically minded. Increasingly the more ambitious providers of MBAs are seeking to make theirs international, but what this means, apart from having an international student body and drawing on their experience as part of learning, is still uncertain.

Despite the rise in the number of MBAs and their international spread, there are important national differences in the value put on them. The importance attached to MBAs will depend upon the relative emphasis on management as compared to professional qualifications and experience. The Germans attach much more importance to the latter than do the British or Americans and other parts of the English-speaking world. They also have many more PhDs amongst their top management. Only a few Japanese universities offer MBAs, though business is more widely taught as an undergraduate subject. Most Japanese companies value the personal qualities of the recruit and the calibre of the university attended rather than the subject. With lifetime employment, managers do not need paper credentials to help them to move companies.

An encouraging aspect of management development today is the new ways in which companies are trying to ensure good education that is relevant to their needs. They are taking a much more active interest than they used to do in the content and quality of the education that their employees receive from outside providers. One fairly recent development is for a company to commission a university to provide a tailored course for its own staff which leads to a certificate, diploma or degree. From the company's point of view this has several advantages: it will be more relevant to the company's needs, both in organization and in content, than a public programme; the participants are less likely to leave and senior management can contribute to the training.

A distinction is sometimes made between training to improve managers' performance in their present job and education for promotion. This distinction can be challenged on the grounds that all management training should be developmental. This is an admirable warning, but large firms may have to judge that one manager is more likely to reach the top than another if they are to give their future top managers sufficient experience on the way up. Some distinctions on promotability are probably necessary, but they can be made without creating a permanent elite.

Those who do distinguish between training to improve performance and education for promotion think of the former as being concerned with technical knowledge and the skills and tools of management, including the ability to write and speak clearly and effectively and to relate well to other people. Training may also include an attempt to change attitudes to management, especially when the organization, like a privatized utility, is undergoing a major cultural change. Education for promotion may be described as 'broadening'.

Broadening, whether thought of solely in relation to promotion or as something that should be the aim of all management education, means a deepening of understanding as well as knowledge of areas beyond one's functional background. Such an understanding should cover three areas. First, the manager must understand the nature of the external environment and its effects on the company, which can range from government regulations and the character of employee relations in the industry, to the general economic situation and the market conditions affecting the firm. In a company with overseas interests, managers may also need to understand something of the economic and social facts in the relevant countries as well as the differences in attitudes to management. Secondly, they must learn to see the business as a whole and the role and problems of each department. Thirdly, their understanding of people's reactions must be deepened, as well as being extended, to include different types of people from those they may have dealt with on the shop floor or in the offices. They will have to learn how to manage managers – both those who work for them and, using the word 'manage' in a different sense, their peers who may be competing with them for promotion, for status, and for scarce resources. Broadening should make managers more aware of all the factors that influence their job and their organization, more aware of their own reactions and more perceptive of other people's and more flexible in their approach. It is one thing to describe in very general terms what is meant by broadening, and another to know how to achieve it, or to know whether there is any good general prescription or only individual ones.

One method used, although not so frequently as it is advocated, is job rotation. Those who favour it argue that it widens managers' experience and should make them more flexible. Some also believe that, if managers are to get the necessary experience for top management, their experience must be planned and accelerated, and that if they are to get quickly enough up the management ladder, they must be singled out for such planned experience. Some companies try to ensure that such managers get an understanding of the business by moving them from one department to another, by sending them to foreign subsidiaries or by putting them in a job that gives them a general view of many aspects of the business.

The use of this planned development is restricted by the price that may have to be paid in temporary dislocation when a person with no knowledge of a department is put into a vacant post in preference to a suitable person already in that department. The companies using job rotation as a conscious policy are likely to have a general policy of moving people in their early years, and later to practise selective job rotation. Some of the very large companies occasionally create vacancies in order to develop those earmarked for top management. For others with potential, suitable vacancies will be used when they arise. Job rotation as a means of developing managers by widening their experience is fairly straightforward, although there is much we do not know about the mechanics, how long should be spent in the different jobs and what kind of transfers between departments are desirable and practicable?

Increasingly management development is also being used as an important means of changing the culture of an organization. This may be done, as it was in some of the privatized utilities in the UK, by sending managers to specially tailored programmes in business schools. It may also be done by re-energizing and redirecting the in-house training school. The most quoted example of the latter is the General Electric's Management Development Institute at Crotonville in the USA.[20] By 1985 the Institute had become a workshop for wrestling with real problems. This was recognized by a new mission statement:

> To leverage GE's global competitiveness, as an instrument of cultural change, by improving the business acumen, leadership abilities and organizational effectiveness of General Electric professionals.[21]

Key transition points in people's careers were identified for development programmes. This has been done before by other companies, but the GE model has more stages than are customary and is worth quoting as an example of the importance attached to continuing and phased development:

- courses for newly recruited graduates that focus on GE values, their values and the meaning of global competition
- new manager development program focusing on people skills
- senior functional program focusing on leadership in their own function and managing change, with change projects
- executive programs consisting of three four-week programmes taken over five to eight years. These include outdoor leadership challenge experiences and consulting team projects
- top management workshops which are held periodically to tackle unresolved, company-wide issues, with the CEO participating.

There are also a variety of elective courses.

There is little evidence about the effects of management education on attitudes. Much of the research on effectiveness of management education is inconclusive, partly because of the great difficulty of finding ways of assessing it. We do know that attitudes can be changed by drastic means, such as the brainwashing of prisoners or the methods used to change the attitudes of a man or woman entering a monastery or a convent. Happily the more common organizations cannot use such drastic methods, but any process of changing attitudes needs to go through three stages. The first is unfreezing of present attitudes so that the individual is ready to change. This can be accomplished either by increasing the pressure to change or by reducing some of the threats or resistance to change. The second stage is the actual change of attitude; when the person learns new attitudes either by identifying with and emulating some person holding these attitudes, or by being placed in a situation where new attitudes are demanded as a way of solving unavoidable problems. The third stage is refreezing, that is, the new attitudes become part of the personality.

Unfreezing of attitudes is easiest where the need for change becomes obvious. A severe competitive threat to a company can help to do that. Often, however, top management is trying to change attitudes without such a strong threat. This is one reason why management courses are held in residential centres, where the manager is isolated from the pressures of daily life, because they are more likely to provide the setting in which a manager may become willing, and able, to change. Much will depend on the atmosphere of the course and the support it gives to efforts at self-examination.

The possibility of any change lasting will depend upon the situation to which managers return. If they go to a different job, or if several of their fellow-managers go on a similar course, there is more chance of it doing so. Job rotation can help to unfreeze attitudes and thus make a change of attitudes easier. A move from one setting to another removes many of the supports of the old attitude, thus giving the manager an opportunity to try new ways of behaving and to be exposed to different attitudes. A special version of putting managers in new settings, which is popular with some companies, is the outdoor course where managers have to cooperate in surmounting the hazards of adventurous outdoor activities.

A course just before a manager goes to a new job provides a better opportunity for learning and modifying attitudes and behaviour than one where the return is to the same job and relationships. A post as personal assistant, where a good relationship develops, will influence younger managers to adopt the attitudes of the older, but they will not learn new methods of looking at management problems. If a broad view is required, rotation to a number of jobs can expose the young manager to a variety of points of view.

The uncertainties about the aims and methods of management education are, or should be, increased by the fact that management consists of so many different jobs and that it is demonstrably possible to manage successfully in many different ways. The very diversity of successful managers must make one pause before offering a general prescription for either what are successful managers or how they should be developed. The research on leadership indicates that one can say, in very general terms, that a good manager is perceptive and flexible and that therefore experience and formal education should be planned to try to develop these qualities.

The move, in some management education, to a more individual approach recognizes the limitations of general lectures to groups of managers, who will differ both in the nature of their jobs and in their styles of learning. A greater emphasis upon the individual's setting and needs can cater for these differences. The interest in promoting self-development encourages individuals to adapt what management writers and teachers have to say to their own needs.

One approach to management education, which has taken many forms, is the provision of real life examples to make education more realistic and practical. The oldest version of this, still popular today, is the case study. But the more radical versions take the student out of the classroom. These include: secondment to another organization; shadowing a senior executive for a day or more; visiting another organization for a day as a group with the task of describing what is different about its culture from their own and why; serving on a junior board, working on projects in, and usually for, an organization. Such methods are a valuable addition to the theory that may be provided by lectures.

A potential danger in some companies' management development is pointed out in Edwin Miller's review of international management development:

There is a danger that those firms which have most successfully articulated and implemented their management development programmes run the risk of shaping their managers so that they act in similar ways and accept the idea there is 'one best way' to approach or handle a problem. ... The pressures of corporate culture are generally towards a common approach to problems, and towards actions, common language and shared values which reinforce the corporation's way of doing business; these pressures may result in inflexibility and discouragement of creativity and innovation.[22]

In saying this, Miller is echoing, though with an international dimension, a best-seller of the 1950s, William H. Whyte's book, *The Organization Man*, which gave a vivid picture of the character and dangers of such conformity.[23]

In all the discussion about management education – and all the vested interests in promoting it – it is easy to forget that management is both a practical art as well as an applied science. That is why it is possible to be a good manager without being educated in management. The hope, for all those whose livelihood depends on buyers for management education, and all those who spend time, and sometimes their own money, on such education, is that education and training can help to make good, or potentially good, managers better, even though it cannot make bad managers good ones.

How important is a good manager?

We have talked so far as if producing good managers is of key importance to the success of a company. In doing so we have mirrored the views of many top managers today. Yet there is a danger that enthusiasm for management selection and development may place too much emphasis on the manager and too little on the organization. We may be trying to find a cure for the failings of management through management education, when our attention ought first to be directed to the organization in which the manager has to work. How managers manage is only partly due to the kind of people they are, for their behaviour is also affected by the position in which they are placed.

Although we must continue to do all we can to improve the selection and training of managers, we should not think of good managers as the sole, or even necessarily the most important, factor in successful management. The culture of the organization, that is, the ways that people customarily behave towards each other, is important in determining how well the organization works. This is more widely recognized today.

Summary

'Leader' is often used instead of 'manager' because it has more appeal. Much of the research into leadership is relevant to managers because leading is one aspect of managing.

The early research into leadership explored three problems: the qualities of leaders, their tasks and what style produces the best performance. The findings show that leadership is more complex and varied than had been expected. There is no one good leader, no one style that works best in all situations and in many groups different people may lead in different ways and at different times. However, there is agreement about the tasks, but at such a general level of description – consideration and getting the work out – that its utility is limited. A good leader should be above average on both, although their relative importance will vary with the kind of job to be done.

The traits and abilities needed to lead people tend to vary from one situation to another. This is the reason why selection of managers is so difficult. There needs to be a match between the manager, the staff and the situation. Democratic leadership is generally more satisfying and effective than autocratic leadership, but there are exceptions. It is important to stress the different leadership requirements for different situations, yet the lists we gave earlier are of the general qualities that the writers thought were necessary.

In many countries, Germany and Japan being the most notable exceptions, the MBA has increasingly been seen as a useful form of management education and a desirable addition to the ambitious manager's CV. The form of MBA has been changing from the predominantly academic, knowledge-based degree, still popular in the USA, to one that combines formal learning with learning by and from experience.

Management education can be divided into the acquisition of specific information and skills and the deepening of understanding. The latter covers three areas: one, an awareness of the external environment of the organization and its effects upon it; two, an understanding of the organization as a whole and of the interrelationships of departments; and, three, a greater insight into people's reactions including one's own. There is a further aim for some internal courses, that of changing attitudes. Unfortunately we know little about how to do that or whether our attempts to do so by education are successful. However, we do know that there first needs to be an unfreezing of present attitudes.

Three anxieties were expressed about management education. One, that too little attention is paid in many programmes to the diversity of jobs and to individual needs and learning styles. Happily, there is a move away from lectures to large groups of managers to a more individual approach that aims to encourage self-development and to the greater use of methods of learning outside the classroom. Two, that management education may be seen as a cure for problems that have their causes in bad organization and a poor working climate. Good managers are not the only factor in successful management. Three, that internal management development may encourage the cloning of managers, what William Whyte in the 1950s famously called the 'organization man'.

Part Two
The Organization

The first two chapters describe the organization within which the manager will have to work. The third looks at the relation between the organization and the people who make it work; how they modify the formal organization as well as how the organization affects the ways in which they think and act.

5 The setting for modern management

Management used to be an easier, more intuitive job than it is today. The vast majority of firms had simple organizations with few managers. Of course, there was specialization, but the division between jobs was often fluid, and the jobs were tailor-made to the individuals available. The sales manager might advise on office management and the works manager might help with the accounts. Relations within management were often informal, so that the foreman could go direct to the managing director with a problem. Rules were few. Decisions were made by hunch based on experience.

Today, the same firm, if it has done even moderately well, will be larger and its organization more complex. The number of managers and specialists will have increased at a faster rate than the number of other employees, thus contributing to the growth in administrative overheads. The management levels will be more numerous and more clearly defined. Specialization of jobs will have increased; the duties of the job may be described in detail together with the qualifications of the person who would be suitable to fill it. Individuals will be fitted to jobs rather than vice versa. Rules will have developed to cover many aspects of the business, such as who is authorized to spend money, how much and on what, or what provision is made when an employee is sick. These rules will apply to categories of people, such as factory managers or manual workers; their application to individuals will depend upon which category they are in.

This brief account of a fair-sized company today could also be used to describe the organization of a hospital, the army or the civil service. It is the description of a bureaucracy. This word is not used disparagingly but with the technical meaning given to it by sociologists for a method of organization that has certain characteristics. These are not only widespread today but also appeared in some earlier civilizations – for instance, in the civil service of ancient China.

Bureaucracy makes possible a rational approach to administration. Hence it develops in any large organization that aims at efficiency and continuity. Increasing size makes orderly administration essential. Smaller companies may still be run successfully just on intuition and drive; in a large company the resulting chaos will be too inefficient.

It may seem strange to say that the reason for the development of bureaucracy is its efficiency, when the word 'bureaucratic' is often used as a synonym for inefficiency; but this refers to possible developments within a bureaucracy and not to its basic characteristics. Even today, with so many changes in organizations, it is still useful to understand the setting within which managers work in any large organization, though some large organizations are more bureaucratic than others.

Why worry about the characteristics of large organizations when most are small? Because large organizations, whether they are companies or in the public sector, employ many more people. Relatively speaking, there are very few large companies but they form an important part of the British and of other developed economies.

Characteristics of bureaucracy

There are four main characteristics, which were described by Weber in 1920.[1] The first is *specialization*. This exists among any group of people working together, but it is highly developed in a bureaucracy. The distinctive feature of specialization in a bureaucracy is that it applies to the job rather than to the individual, so that the job usually continues in existence when the present holder leaves. This makes for continuity. The functions of the job are defined; therefore, the qualifications of the individual who could fill it are, to some extent, specified. The jobholder must have the experience and education required for that post.

The second common feature of all bureaucracies is the *hierarchy of authority*, which makes a sharp distinction between the administrators and the administered. In industry it is between management and workers, in the armed services between the officers and the rank and file. Within the ranks of administrators there are also clearly defined levels of authority. This detailed and precise stratification is very marked in the armed forces and the civil service. It exists in many large organizations, where both the levels of authority and the rewards at each level are laid down.

The third characteristic of bureaucracy, the *system of rules*, is closely related to the fourth, *impersonality*, since the aim of the rules is an efficient and impersonal operation. The rules are more or less stable, although of course, some of them will be changed or modified with time. They can be learned, and knowledge of them is one of the requisites of holding a job in a bureaucracy. The existence of these rules is in marked contrast to more informal organizations.

Impersonality is the characteristic distinguishing bureaucracy most clearly from other types of organization: for example, from that based on kinship, which is found in primitive societies and to a lesser extent in civilized societies in, say, some family firms. The allocation of privileges is impersonal in a bureaucracy, as is the exercise of authority, which should be in accordance with the rules laid down and not arbitrary. Hence, in the more highly developed bureaucracies there tend to be carefully defined procedures for appealing against certain types of decisions – the bureaucracy must not only be impersonal but must be seen to be impersonal.

It is the demand for impersonality, the operation of the rules without ill-will and without favour, which makes the acceptance of bribes a cardinal sin for the Western bureaucrat. It is also the reason why unscheduled privilege is viewed with such disfavour and why rules to try to prevent privilege based on favouritism are so carefully developed. This does not, of course, mean that there are no privileges for officials in a bureaucracy, but what there are must be allocated according to definite rules based on rank or seniority. The transition, from the personal bestowal of privileges at the discretion of senior managers to their allocation according to rules, can be seen in many businesses. Nor is it often an easy one. The exact definition of the levels entitled to certain privileges, such as an allocated parking space or a particular grade of car, can cause many heartaches among those seeking for the privilege, and headaches among the personnel officers trying to define unquestionable rules for its allocation. One of the modern trends is to reduce some of the management status privileges. This is most marked in eating places. In the past many large companies had different levels of dining rooms for junior, middle and top management; now a common canteen or an open choice between a self-service canteen and waitress service has increasingly taken their place.

Demands for equality of treatment has been one of the reasons for the growth of bureaucracy. The strength of the demand is influenced by the ideology prevailing at that time and place. It is less strong in Britain than it was but it is still important. Citizens want equality of treatment from the civil service, and questions in the House try to ensure that they get it, thereby putting pressure on civil servants to administer strictly in accordance with the rules, so that no questions will be asked. Employees, through their union, strive for the acceptance of rules to ensure that management cannot discriminate between individuals at its own discretion.

When fairness is identified with equality of treatment, variations in the conditions of work within one large organization are likely to be challenged as unfair. If rules and procedures that are demonstrably fair by this standard are to be devised, little or no allowance can be made for local difficulties and preferences. The increasing realization of the limitations imposed by equality of treatment has led to the idea of a menu of the contents of a reward package from which employees can make choices to suit their own needs and interests.

The power of those who complain of inequality of treatment to bring pressure upon senior officials is important in determining the extent to which rules are made to ensure impersonal treatment. Civil service rules are the most carefully devised. The client and the employee when they are organized to demand equality of treatment both exert pressure towards greater bureaucracy. Yet, being human and therefore paradoxical, they may complain of bureaucracy when these rules are applied to themselves, and condemn an unfeeling machine that takes no account of individuals.

The four characteristics of a bureaucracy, *specialization, a hierarchy of authority, a system of rules and impersonality,* have developed because they are the most efficient method yet discovered of running a large and continuing organization. They make for efficiency partly because they ensure the continuity essential for any organization that is to last longer than the life of its founder; and partly because they provide, as far as possible, for management to be carried out on a rational basis by the development of a logical system of rules, of division of work, of qualifications for office, and of defined levels of authority. The scope for human whims is reduced to a minimum.

Bureaucracy has developed because it is more efficient than other forms of organization. It makes for rational and continuing administration. The increasing size and complexity of organizations encourage the growth of bureaucracy. So does the demand for equality of treatment. Rapid change limits the growth of bureaucracy because a more flexible organization is needed to adapt to it, hence some argue that bureaucracy is out of date.

Limitations on the growth of bureaucracy

There are two main limitations on the growth of bureaucracy. The first is management attitudes and philosophy and the second the pressure of rapid change. These help to explain why even large organizations differ in the extent of their bureaucracy.

Management attitudes and philosophy

We have seen powerful reasons why managers of large companies should make them more bureaucratic. The extent to which they do so will depend partly on their attitude to management and the kind of people they are and partly on the situation of their companies. Some managers dislike the orderly administration characteristic of a bureaucracy. They may find it irksome, even unbearably so, to be bound by the rules. They may attach great value to intuition and initiative. They may prefer to reward where they think fit, paying the salary that they think the individual is worth and giving the privileges that they think are deserved. They may trust their own judgement in selection and expect individuals to mould the jobs to suit themselves, rather than choose a person to fit a job specification. In sum, they may believe that initiative is only fostered in a freewheeling company, where people are able to enlarge their jobs and to earn as much as they prove themselves to be worth.

The attitudes and personality of top management will therefore influence the amount of bureaucracy in the company. But even if management is opposed to bureaucracy, there are, as we have seen, powerful pressures towards it, which makes it difficult for a large company to prosper without a bureaucratic framework.

The prevailing management philosophy will influence management actions. Earlier the emphasis was on the technical advantages to be derived from size and from making use of the most qualified expert. Now there is greater concern for human reactions, for choosing the right people and giving them more freedom to manage.

Pressure of change

An organization in a rapidly changing situation cannot, if it is to be successful, be very bureaucratic; jobs change, authority relationships become more flexible and many of the rules cease to be appropriate. Therefore, the situation in which the organization operates will influence the amount of bureaucracy that is possible. The rapid change that has affected many organizations in recent years has necessarily led to a decline in the amount of bureaucracy. So has the move to create smaller semi-autonomous units within larger organizations.

Managers in a bureaucracy

What are the implications for junior and middle managers of working in a large organization today? It will have both advantages and disadvantage for them, and fewer advantages for the managers who prefer to do their own thing. Managers will be appointed for their qualifications rather than for their connections. The greater the belief in the need for qualifications, the smaller becomes the personal element in appointment. This will suit young managers who are looking for a post and are short of connections. They may be less enthusiastic when they want to appoint new staff and find that their freedom is restricted by the appointments procedure.

Managers in a bureaucracy are expected to be loyal to the organization rather than to a person. In return the organization looks after them as long as they fulfil their duties. What is meant by 'fulfilling one's duties' varies considerably, but in some British businesses security of tenure, and established career expectations, used to be nearly as great for managers as for the established civil servant. In both business and the civil service, but particularly in the former, there is more insecurity today.

One of the great advantages for managers of working in a bureaucracy is that they are free from much former arbitrariness. They will know much better where they stand in the organization. Their responsibilities and authority will be laid down. Good work will be more likely to be rewarded by promotion, since bureaucracies try to make an impersonal assessment of merit. Privileges and, to some extent, pay will be determined by the post occupied rather than by their standing with their bosses. However, the flexibility and secrecy of salaries which still exists in some companies is one of the ways in which they are unbureaucratic.

In a bureaucracy greater emphasis is placed on the value of professional skill, on a rational, matter-of-factness. This means that managers must be able to convince others of the correctness of their judgement. However, being human their willingness to be convinced will depend partly on whether they get on well with them.

One of the disadvantages for managers of working in a bureaucracy is that their freedom of action will be curtailed. They will be restricted by the definition of their job's responsibilities and authority. They are the occupant of a continuing post that has certain duties and privileges attached to it. They must manage within the rules of the organization and accept the limitations on their authority, including their authority over their staff. Some managers will consider these disadvantages a small price to pay for greater security and steady advancement by merit; others may reluctantly adjust to this form of management or devote part of their energy to finding ways of evading the rules and increasing their freedom of action. Yet others will choose to work in a less bureau-cratic, more freewheeling, company where their chances of rapid promotion may be greater.

The problems of bureaucracy

The problems of bureaucracy are the problems of balance. The characteristics of bureaucracy: specialization, hierarchy of authority, a system of rules and impersonality, help to make for efficient and continuing organizations but only if they are not developed to excess. There are two main dangers: one, that what should only be means become ends in them-selves; two, that insufficient allowance is made for different or for changing conditions.

The classic danger in a bureaucracy is of course an overem-phasis on rules; hence the stereotype of a bureaucrat as a man who punctiliously keeps to formal procedures however inappropriate – the man who hoists the flag while the building is burning. The existence of rules inevitably limits flexibility. One reason why 'bureaucratic' is often a slur word is because a bureaucracy is necessarily impersonal in administration of its rules and is often accused of inhumanity. Hence one of the problems of a bureaucracy is how to combine the development of impersonal rules that prevent favouritism with sufficient flexibility to deal with the hard case that does not fit the rules. Impersonality can be modified by the way in which the rules are devised, so that some latitude is left to the managers in interpreting them to meet a hard case. Bureaucracies must be impersonal, but the individuals in them can strive to be humane in their interpretation of the rules and in the way they behave to others.

Another obvious danger of bureaucracy is rigidity; hence an inability to adapt fast enough to changing conditions. This is most likely in a company where the managers are used to stable conditions and now find that their old methods are unsuited to a changing market. By the late 1990s the large majority of managers have had to adjust to rapidly changing conditions, so few now have to face the traumas that existed for managers who had been used to stability. An extreme example of this was the director of a whisky company interviewed in the early 1960s who was asked: 'What have been the main changes that were made in the last two years?' Longish pause for thought, then the reply: 'Well, a year ago we redesigned the label'.

Yet another potential weakness of bureaucracy is the development of managerial clones. Any organization must try to ensure that its members further its objectives, and will seek to do so by the use of discipline, incentives, and by encouraging a sense of loyalty to the organization and a devotion to duty. This is most marked in the armed services. The problem, especially in industry and commerce where innovation is often essential, is to do this without developing an organization type to which all newcomers are expected to conform. Again it is a problem of balance, since there will always be a clash between the need for managers to be reliable and the dangers of over-conformity. Top management should assess whether it has the balance right between the advantages of reliability and the limitations of conformity. In weighing the scales it should allow for the fact that judgement is likely to be weighted against the individualist.

A particular danger of a governmental bureaucracy is the volume of paper that results from the requirement to keep records for accountability and the tendency to play safe. As one manager, who was new to the ways of Whitehall, put it: 'Here the people feel a need to protect themselves by sending every minute that they write to everyone who could conceivably have an interest. The result is that the noise in the system is such that the signal gets lost.'

Despite the weaknesses of bureaucracies, the conclusions from our discussion are that the characteristics of a bureaucracy are bound to develop in an established and continuing organization that seeks to be efficient. Nor can they be avoided in a government department that is accountable to Parliament. Even in companies some degree of bureaucracy is essential for efficient management. The problem is how much? As organizations grow, they need to become more bureaucratic to ensure order in what is done, but the inherent dangers of bureaucracy need to be guarded against. A knowledge of what these are can help to prevent them. The amount of bureaucracy that is appropriate will vary with the particular circumstances of the organization. What these are, and how they do, and should, influence the organization and the behaviour of management will be a recurring subject throughout this book. A general guide is that the greater the rate of change affecting the organization, the more adaptable it needs to be, and hence the less formal and bureaucratic.

Bureaucracy outmoded?

The discussion so far may seem incredibly old-fashioned. Modern books on management are not about bureaucracy, but about new forms of organization for a rapidly changing world. It is true that we have seen major changes in large organizations, reflected in ugly new words like delayering, downsizing and re-engineering. New forms and shapes of organizations have been heralded by phrases like the federal organization and the network organization. But does this mean that bureaucracy is outmoded? That organizations have changed so radically that the bureaucratic characteristics described above no longer exist? A series of meetings in the early 1990s in the USA tried to find the answer by examining what the new post-bureaucractic organization might look like.

The editors of the papers at these meetings point to long-standing developments that potentially undermine bureaucracy, such as self-managing work teams and the sharing of information that used to be held only at the top. The similarity that they see in all these developments is that they put more emphasis on relations based on influence rather relations based on power. However, they conclude:

> The search for an alternative to bureaucracy is almost as old as the concept itself. . . . Yet the truth is that although many companies have joined in the anti-bureaucratic rhetoric, few have actually moved more than a step or two from traditional structures.[2]

What a contrast these findings are to all the talk about revolutionary changes in organizations! In the same volume, Nohria and Berkeley point out that:

Weber's principles of bureaucratic organization continue to serve as benchmarks for our understanding of the contemporary work organization.[3]

What it is also useful to understand is that more organizations today contain mainly, or a considerable number of, professionals. Management of such organizations, whether they are partnerships of lawyers, architects or accountants, or organizations such as the National Health Service with a large professional staff, is different from that of most manufacturing companies and commercial companies like retail chain stores. An organization employing many professionals will still have bureaucratic features but there is less reliance on control through rules and regulations and more on professional discretion and self-regulation, so trust is more important. Management must be good at negotiation, bargaining and collective decision-making and will require more diplomatic skills, because professionals resist direction. It requires too 'the talent to invent what makes work and careers interesting and challenging'.[4]

Summary

Bureaucracy provides a common setting – and one we often take for granted – for organizations with different purposes. ('Bureaucracy' was used with its sociological meaning of a particular form of organization, not in its pejorative sense.) The characteristics of a bureaucracy, which these organizations have in common, are: one, *specialization* of jobs, which become continuing posts for which suitably qualified individuals are recruited; two, *a hierarchy of authority* composed of clearly defined levels; three, *a system of rules;* and four, *impersonality,* which is seen both in the administration of the rules and in selection and promotion.

For managers there are advantages and disadvantages in working in a bureaucracy. It suits some temperaments better than others. On the one hand, managers are freed from much former arbitrariness. They will be appointed for their experience and qualifications and, as far as possible, promoted on merit. They will have an established status with appropriate salary and privileges. They can, though much less so than in the past, look forward to a known pattern of career expectations. Their loyalty should be to the organization rather than to individuals. On the other hand, managers lose some of their freedom of action. They will be the occupant of a continuing position with prescribed duties and constraints within which they must work. If they are good, their speed of advancement may be less than in a more freewheeling organization.

The problems of bureaucracy are the problems of balance – how to have rules that are impersonal but not inhuman, that are fair yet take the individual into account; how to have a structure that is not too rigid to adjust to change; how to have loyal managers who further the organization's objectives without developing into organization men and women. These problems are inescapable, but they can be ameliorated.

Modern management writers focus on the many changes taking place in organizations. They talk about new forms of organization, hence a discussion of bureaucracy seems too old-fashioned to be worthwhile. Yet a series of meetings in the USA in the early 1990s, which examined whether they could identify the post-bureaucratic organization, concluded that few companies have moved more than a step or two from traditional structures. The main change that might in time lead to new forms of organization are the different developments that together will mean that relationships come to be based more on influence than on power. Meanwhile the characteristics of bureaucracy do still help us to understand the contemporary work organization.

6 What kind of structure?

Any manager needs to understand the main problems to be tackled in designing the formal structure of an organization. Few will have to plan a new organization but many will have some opportunities to make choices in how work is to be organized. They will benefit from knowing the pros and cons of different choices. So will managers who are having to cope with a reorganization, which is a common experience for most managers in large organizations. Understanding what is happening can help to reduce the stress. Being able to predict the likely consequences of an organizational change helps in managing it.

There are three aspects to an organization. There is the formal structure, which can be shown on an organization chart; there are the policies and procedures; and, more important than these two, there is people's behaviour within the organization. 'More important' because what people do will determine how well the organization works in practice. Yet the formal structure and the policies and procedures do matter, because they help to determine the kinds of jobs that people have, how they feel about their work, how easy it is to coordinate people's activities, and whether cooperation or conflict are encouraged.

This chapter is limited to the formal structure of the organization. It aims to:

1 Describe the main problems of organization and the kinds of decisions that have to be made in planning the structure.
2 Discuss what has been learnt from the study of structures in organizations and what relevance this has for the manager.

We saw in the last chapter that the characteristics of a bureaucracy still exist today, to a greater or lesser extent, in all large organizations and in most medium-sized ones, too. Yet they only provide the setting within which the organization will be designed. A hierarchy of authority and specialization of jobs are but the beginning. They do not provide the answer to two of the main problems of organization: how the work is to be divided – both between posts at the same levels and between different levels – and how it is to be coordinated. Once work is divided, there has to be coordination.

In any kind of organization, be it a company, a government department, a public agency, a hospital, a school or a charity, decisions have to be made about what work is to be done, how it is to be divided between jobs, and how jobs are to be grouped into sections, departments and even larger groupings. What kind of jobs to establish is so important a decision that it is discussed in a separate chapter in the companion volume, *The Reality of Organizations*.[1] Here we shall look at the broader questions of the main types of work to be done and of how these are to be grouped together.

Division of work

The first decision in a new organization is what are the main functions to be performed. In any company there are some obvious divisions. In a manufacturing company these will be production, marketing and sales, finance and personnel. Other functions are essential in some industries but not in others. A research department, for example, is vital to a company in a highly technical industry. New functions get added as organizations change or as new technology provides new ways of dealing with existing tasks. Computers and office technology are an example of how new technology can affect the division of work. There are more specialized examples, such as intensive care wards in hospitals.

The work of an organization is divided into the main functions, such as production and sales in a company, and into staff or specialist jobs. The main functions are called line because they have direct responsibility for achieving the objectives of the organization. The support functions, such as human resource management, are called staff. Whether a function is line or staff should depend on the organization's objectives. Research, for instance, is sometimes line when new products and processes are vital for the success of the company, or staff when its role is less important.

There are often problems in establishing satisfactory relations between line and staff personnel. These are less difficult than they used to be because many staff personnel have been made directly responsible to line managers instead of being in a separate department. It is most commonly in human resource management that the old problems remain of the staff people feeling frustrated by their lack of responsibility and frequent inability to get their ideas put into effect.

Satisfactory relations between line managers and staff personnel can only be achieved with time, which allows for the growth of mutual confidence. Hence, when management is planning a new organization, it cannot provide an answer to the problems of the relations between the two. It can, however, minimize the likelihood of trouble. The staff specialists should be located as near as possible to the managers they are serving, so that mutual confidence can have the best chance of developing.

What work should be done within the organization and what should be done outside by using other firms specializing in that kind of work or individual consultants? This choice has become so prominent today that a new word has been coined for it: 'outsourcing'. Market research, public relations, transport, catering, cleaning and computing are examples of services required in many organizations that are now often bought from outside. Now some organizations are going much further. In 1996, for example, British Airways announced that it was outsourcing many of its activities. The further outsourcing goes the more key becomes the question: 'what is the organization's real role, that is what would it not consider contracting out?' A 1996 survey of several hundred companies by PA Consulting Group in London found that a quarter of their budgets for their key business processes were outsourced. There were only three activities that more than a third of the companies saw as their core: business strategy, information technology strategy and new product development.[2]

Peters and Waterman's well-known advice, 'stick to the knitting'[3] may be one reason for the growth of outsourcing as it may have helped top management to explore whether some of the things that are done in-house could be done cheaper and better by a specialist firm. Another reason is the opportunities that information technology provides for linking those who are working from home. It makes for the revival of the cottage industry in its modern electronic form. Yet another, and important, reason is that a reduction in the number of employees gives greater flexibility to adjust to declining demand.

Grouping of work

In a simple organization it may be easy to decide what jobs should be grouped together, as the division of work between the major activities is clear. Production, sales and accounts will be needed in a simple manufacturing company. It is only as organizations get larger that choices have to be made. In sales, for example, a common choice is between organizing by product, with sales staff responsible for particular products, or by area, when the sales force is organized geographically. Organization by area is a common basis in government departments dealing directly with the public. The type of customer or client is another common basis for dividing up work. In companies there may be separate sales staff for important customers. In hospitals patients may be grouped together by sex, age, type of illness or the amount of care required.

How many tiers?

The number of tiers in the management hierarchy varies in practice from two in a small company to eight or even more in some large organizations. Size obviously makes a difference, but management still has considerable choice as to how many levels to establish. It may opt for as few tiers as possible, on the grounds that this makes for better communication, more responsible and interesting jobs and improves efficiency. The more complex the organization – and many tiers is one aspect of complexity – the more time will be consumed in organizational as distinct from operational work.

One of the major changes in large organizations in recent years has been a cut, often a considerable one, in the number of tiers. A survey by the Conference Board in the USA, published in 1995, found that 28 per cent of the companies surveyed reported no more than four layers of management, whereas five years earlier only 8 per cent of the respondents said that they had as few as that. Only 10 per cent of the companies in the most recent survey, compared with 40 per cent five years earlier, said that they had eight or more layers of management between line workers and the chief executive.[4] These figures show the extent of 'delayering', which has been so talked about. Even so, there remain sufficient tiers to create the problems that are discussed in Chapter 9 on large organizations.

It is easier to cut the number of management tiers in a business that lends itself to the creation of smaller, semi-autonomous units than one which requires large plants. However, the dramatic changes in the organization of mass car manufacture – learning from the Japanese – showed that the lower management tiers could be eliminated by creating partially self-governing work teams.

The number of tiers will determine the span of control, that is, the number of people reporting directly to a manager. The larger the number the less detailed supervision and personal coordination of subordinates' work is possible. This does not matter if standard procedures can reduce the need for personal supervision and the staffs' work does not interlock. Retail chain store managers are an example of both, so that the regional manager can be in charge of a large number of individual chain store managers. Effective work teams that do much of their own supervision and coordination also make fewer tiers possible, so do the developments in computer-based information.

Organization charts

Management should next decide whether it wants an organization chart and, if so, what kind. It might consider some of the attempts that have been made to draw charts that are more informative than the traditional ones. If its planning has been as methodical as our description, it will probably have roughed out a chart as it went along. The chart helps to show what has been devised. It will also be useful for showing to newly appointed managers and inquiring visitors. But organization charts have their dangers. Their usefulness is often exaggerated and they can rapidly get out of date. All too few organizations charts have explanatory notes; without them, readers may make different assumptions about their meaning. They may also be in danger of thinking the reality is as tidy as the chart (in the next chapter we shall see how far the two may be divorced). Unless charts are frequently revised, they may soon give a false picture of even the formal organization. In sum, an organization chart can be a useful tool, and an aid to explanation about the organization, but it is often misused. Its apparent clarity can be misleading.

At this stage in planning an organization the framework is complete, but the task is not finished. If, for instance, top management interviews a potential sales manager and shows the chart, the question that might and should be asked is: 'How much responsibility shall I have?' This question would show up two areas that have yet to be tackled. One, what type of decisions should be taken at each level of management – that is, how much decentralization should there be? Two, what should be the responsibilities of each job?

Decentralization

One of the most difficult decisions to be made in planning or in changing an organization is how much decentralization there should be. No organization of any size is completely centralized, for if it is to work at all, some decisions must be taken on the spot rather than at the centre. The choice is not between centralization and decentralization but of how much decentralization there should be and what decisions should be made at different levels. The answer is likely to vary from one company to another, according to what decisions top management consider of vital importance to the business. In one company, for example, all proposed price changes have to be referred to top management. In another, pricing decisions will be made lower down.

What is the best balance between centralization and decentralization may well vary at different periods in a firm's history. In a new company, or in an amalgamation of two or more companies, greater centralization will be necessary in the early stages so as to establish common policies, where these are desired. A well-established management tradition will make greater decentralization easier, because managers will tend to think and act in the same way. The calibre of junior and middle management will also affect the amount of decentralization that is practicable. This is often one of the constraints on decentralization in developing countries. The structure of the company will help to encourage or discourage decentralization. A flat organization will encourage it because responsibility will be divided between fewer levels and because managers with many staff will have to leave more decisions to them.

Discussion of how much decentralization is desirable used to be mainly relevant in companies. The public sector had developed such firm structures that there was much less change. No longer – much of the public sector has been privatized and what remains has often been radically reorganized. The aim has been devolution, and where possible competition, within the constraints of accountability to ministers.

Job descriptions

A subject on which top management in one company may differ from that in another is the extent to which it is desirable to define the responsibilities of a job ('job description') and to specify the qualifications necessary to fill the particular job ('job specification'). At one extreme, top management might appoint a general sales manager and just leave it to him or her to sell the products. At the opposite extreme, before looking for a general sales manager, management draws up a careful job description and from that prepares a specification of the kind of person needed to fill it.

One argument for the first approach, that is, leaving the scope of the job up to the individual, is that if you appoint people with initiative, they will be able to make their own jobs and should not be limited in doing so by being given precise terms of reference. This argument is reinforced for jobs held by professionals and other well-qualified individuals. Another argument for the first approach is that in most companies conditions are always changing; therefore, any attempt to define precisely the responsibilities attached to jobs is bound to become rapidly outdated. Yet another is that as people work more in teams it is inappropriate to define individual job responsibilities. Those who support the second approach argue that definition of responsibilities is essential if top management is to make certain that no aspect of the work is overlooked because nobody is clearly responsible for doing it. It is also suggested that much personal friction can be avoided if people know exactly what they are responsible for and to whom.

The difference in these two approaches reflects a difference in management philosophy. Detailed job descriptions will be supported by those who believe in the virtues of order and of control. The other approach will be favoured by those who emphasize initiative and flexibility. The relative importance of these priorities will vary with the purposes and current position of the organization. Some organizations require more flexibility than others. Even so, top management will tend to favour one approach or the other, though in exercising their preference they will be constrained, as we shall see later, by the rate of change affecting the organization.

Reorganization

So far we have mainly discussed the organizational decisions that must be made when planning a new company. It is easier to describe the kind of decisions that have to be made then. Yet the establishment of a new company that is large enough to have a formal management structure is unusual. The reorganization of existing companies is much more common, and many of the same considerations will apply.

All of them will have to be examined if a really thorough reorganization is being planned. Companies change as they seek to anticipate and to respond to external changes: they may expand, change their products, develop new markets overseas, establish alliances with foreign companies, acquire other companies, and so on. Any or all of these may be reasons why the existing organization no longer seems satisfactory. Many companies have grown piecemeal, often, at least to some extent, around personalities. The posts that were developed by the abilities and weaknesses of particular people may continue after they have left. At times in a company's development, management will feel a need to re-examine the organization..

It is not only companies that have periodic reorganizations. Growth or decline can necessitate a reorganization in other bodies. Many public organizations are changed because their new political masters have different views about what they should be doing. In any type of organization top management may decide that a change must surely be an improvement on the all too visible problems of the present organization. Then, as in the company that is being planned before it is established, management may ask the question: 'What principles, or at least guidelines, are there in planning an efficient organization?' and perhaps, even more specifically: 'Is there a best way of organizing?' This is one of the questions that social scientists answered back in the 1950s and 1960s.

What social scientists have contributed

The approach of social scientists to the study of organizations is almost bewilderingly varied. As Mason Haire pointed out years ago, a parallel would be the fable of the blind men describing an elephant:

> There is little doubt here that it is a single elephant being discussed, but, by and large, each of the observers begins the description from a different point, and often with a special end in view. Each of the authors is dealing with organizations and how they work; but, to some extent, they start from different bases and have different things in mind which need explaining.[5]

This remains true today. What has changed are the aspects of organizations that interest social scientists. In part this reflects the major changes affecting both business in an increasingly globally competitive world, and the public sector as politicians seek to find more economic ways of providing public services. In part it reflects fashion and the particular interests of the current management gurus. The variety of academic interest in organizations has a practical value for the manager. It shows that one can, and should, think about organizations in different ways.

The discussion in this chapter has been about one aspect of organizations, the formal structure. This is no longer a fashionable subject for academics, but for managers there are practical decisions to be made about the structure of work so it is still of relevance. Social scientists' research in the 1950s, 1960s and 1970s contributed to our under-standing of the structure of organizations by showing that there is not one best way to design an organization because different situations require different types of organization. This was a radical change from the received wisdom up to and including the 1950s. Then management pundits like Urwick,[6] whose work was respected on both sides of the Atlantic, looked for and described universal principles that could be applied in designing any organization. Now organization textbooks do not offer universal principles, though some suggest guidelines. This change originated in the studies by social scientists of how organizations work in practice, which showed that universal principles are not valid.

The idea of span of control is a good example of the move from a principle to a guideline. This was Urwick's eighth principle of organizing: 'No person should supervise more than five, or at the most, six direct staff whose work interlocks.'

The argument used to support it was that no individual could understand the relations between more than five or six people if their work was related. However, studies showed that in practice there was a wide range in the number of staff reporting to a manager.

The burden imposed on managers by a particular number of staff reporting to them, and others who have access to them, depends on a great variety of factors, including: temperamental characteristics, such as the extent to which they can be frequently interrupted without becoming upset; questions of ability both of the superior and of the staff; the physical location; the nature of the work, including the type and frequency of the decisions that have to be made; the management information that is readily available and the development of team-working. The latter can reduce the pressure on the manager, as staff may coordinate much of the work themselves.

The phrase 'span of control' is itself questionable, as it suggests the need for much more direct supervision than may be necessary. Staff may be experienced, well motivated and capable of coordinating much of their own work. Their boss may need to spend very little time with them and then mainly for the exchange of information. The role that the boss needs to play in relation to staff is one of the factors that is relevant to deciding how many direct staff would be too many.

The number of people who should report to the chief executive needs special consideration because of its effects on the status of a function. The arguments for a large number of people reporting directly to the chief executive are that:

- each will feel that they are judged to be important enough to do so
- the chief executive will more easily get a picture of what is happening in each directorate
- it will be difficult, if not impossible, to interfere in detail.

The arguments for a smaller number are:

- some directorates will be more crucial to the success of the organization than others, so the chief executive's attention should be focused on those
- a small top group can more easily provide the coherent momentum that is required
- the chief executive will have more time to spend on external relations.

These are the arguments. What happens in practice will depend upon the chief executive's management philosophy. It will also depend upon what is of particular interest. Some chief executives for example are very interested in information technology and would want the head to report directly, others would hate that! Since reporting direct is a signal of the importance the chief executive attaches to that function, he or she will want to show what they consider important. Yet other reasons will affect the decision, such as whether the chief executive is happiest working with a small team. The decision that the chief executive makes about who reports directly is a very personal one resulting in wide differences, even amongst chief executives of divisions within the same organization.

Two studies in the UK in the 1950s and early 1960s, the first by Joan Woodward and the second by Tom Burns and G. M. Stalker, helped to shatter the idea that there are universal principles of organizing. Their most important contribution to our understanding of organizations is showing that different types of business need different forms of organization and that the appropriate kind of organization can change with the company's situation.

Joan Woodward studied 100 manufacturing firms in SE Essex and found a great variety of types of organization.[7] She concluded that the variation could be explained by the type of production. The three main methods – unique and small batch, mass, and process – all needed their own distinctive forms of organization. Even more influential in terms of its impact on thinking about organizational stuctures has been the study by Burns and Stalker. They compared companies in the electronics industry that were going through a rapid change with a firm producing rayon filament yarn, which had become a routine production. This comparison suggested that the amount of change affecting the organization influenced the extent of its flexibility. The research workers distinguished two contrasting types of organization: one they called 'mechanistic', which means suitable for stable conditions; the other 'organic', which means adapted to changing conditions. The firm making rayon filament yarn was an example of a mechanistic organization; in it each person:

> ... knew just what he could do in normal circumstances without consulting anyone else; just what point of deviation from the normal he should regard as the limit of his

competence; and just what he should do when this limit was reached – i.e. report to his superior. The whole system was devised to preserve normality and stability. The downward flow of instructions and orders, and the upward flow of reports and requests for such instructions and orders, were precisely and clearly channelled; it had the characteristics of a smoothly working automatic machine. Since everyone knew both his job and its limits, there was little consultation; contacts ran up and down, from staff to superior and vice versa, and the great majority of those contacts resulted in the giving of definite orders. The outstanding characteristics of the structure was that it was mechanical and authoritarian. And it worked very well.[8]

In stable conditions, such as those operating in this company, the organization can be treated as a mechanical structure. In it each job has precisely defined rights and duties and technical requirements. The knowledge of the firm's needs and situation is concentrated at the top, thus making possible a hierarchic, authoritarian form of management structure. When a company is operating in conditions of rapid change, as the large majority of companies are today, it must be much more flexible and have what Burns and Stalker called an organic system: that is, one in which the boundaries of jobs are fluid and there is more consultation and exchange of information than commands. Interaction between people also takes place laterally as much as vertically. Each of these types of organization suits its different conditions.

Later research by Lawrence and Lorsch made a further contribution to what is now called 'contingency theory', that is, the theory that the nature of the organization is contingent upon its situation.[9] They examined the effect of different environments, in particular the amount of instability and variety, upon the structure and working of organizations. They showed that the nature of the environment affected two organizational tasks, that of *differentiation* between tasks and that of the *integration* of the separate tasks or functions. They found that in complex and dynamic environments there was a greater need for differentiation than in simpler, more stable ones, and the greater the differentiation, the more complex had to become the methods of integration. Greater differentiation of functions led to differences in the attitudes and behaviour of managers in each function. They had different objectives, different time orientations and generally dealt with their colleagues in different ways. Lawrence and Lorsch's study is an illustration of the way in which the structure of the organization affects the behaviour of individuals, a subject that we shall examine in the next chapter.

What these and other research reports indicate is that there is no one ideal form of organization; hence no universally applicable set of principles, except of the most general kind. The organization will vary according to the needs of the company, which will depend upon its situation. Management, therefore, needs to examine the company's objectives, and its current situation, before designing or changing the pattern of organization. This is true for management in any kind of organization.

An example of another early study, which has become a classic because it is still useful today, is that by Herbert Simon and three colleagues. They sought to expand our knowledge about human behaviour in organizations, and to do this in a way that would cast light on the specific problems of organizing effectively the controller's department in large companies.[10] ('Controller' is the American term for the head of the accounting department.) They defined an effective accounting department as one that provided information of high quality, did so at a minimum cost, and facilitated the long-range development of competent accounting executives. The research workers studied seven large companies that were geographically dispersed. These were in a variety of industries and differed in the extent to which they centralized or decentralized their accounting departments. The research was carried out by interviews, by studying accounting reports and, to a limited extent, by observation.

The research workers found that in each of the companies accounting information was used at various levels to answer three different kinds of question: one, scorecard, 'how am I doing?'; two, attention-directing, 'what problems shall I look into?'; and three, problem-solving, 'which course of action is better?' The type of information needed varied at different levels of the organization. The extent to which the information was used depended mainly on how close was the relation between the accountants as sources of information and the managers as consumers. To achieve this close relation, different patterns of organization were needed for the different types of information.

The research showed that there is no such general thing as accounting information. Therefore, in designing the organization of an accounting department one must think of a number of types of data that need different channels of communication if they are to be most useful. The research team concluded that there are three major divisions in the accounting function, each of which can be separated from the others. These are record-keeping, current analysis, and special studies for problem-solving purposes. The research workers said that:

> Combining the functions leads to a potential conflict between the accountant's function of providing service to operating department, and his function of analysing operations to provide valid and objective data for higher levels of management. Separating the record-keeping functions from analytical work is also an important supplement to an effective internal audit in reducing the dangers of collusion. It may also give the analytical personnel greater freedom to develop close working relationships with operating executives without a feeling of conflicting responsibilities.
>
> Another reason for separating the functions is to allow greater flexibility for organizing each of them in the most economical and effective manner. . . . Each can be centralized or decentralized to the extent that appears desirable, independently of the others.[11]

The above is an example of a study with practical applications. It shows how the organization should be designed to meet the needs of those concerned.

Once the idea of universal principles for good organization had been disproved, the search was on to map what kinds of organization suit different conditions. The distinction between mechanistic and organic made by Burns and Stalker has endured, but more elaborate ones have been developed to try to do justice to the variety of organizations that exist. Derek Pugh and David Hickson, as part of the Aston research programme, identified two major structural characteristics that distinguished between the organizations that they studied.[12] One was the extent to which activities were structured with many standardized written procedures and precisely specialized tasks. The other was the concentration of authority with centralized decision-making. From these two structural characteristics they identified four types of organization:

1 *Full bureaucracy*, where activities are both highly structured and decision-making centralized.
2 *Workflow bureaucracy*, with precisely programmed work so that little direct managerial intervention is needed.
3 *Personnel bureaucracy*, where structuring is low but authority is concentrated.
4 *Non-bureaucracy*, which relies on informal relationships.

Henry Mintzberg produced a different kind of typology, which suggested that all organizations have common components but that their importance varies in different kinds of organization.[13] The common components are:

1 The *strategic apex*, that is the top management.
2 The *operating core*, which does the daily work of the organization.
3 The *middle line*, which acts as the communication channel between top management and the operating core.
4 *Technostructure*, which is responsible for standardizing work processes.
5 *Support staff.*

The importance of each of these varies in the five different types of organizations that he distinguished:

1 *Simple structure*, typically a small firm, where top management supervises the day-to-day work processes, so the strategic apex is the most important group.
2 *Machine bureaucracy*, in mass assembly industries, where the technostucture is the most powerful because it deals with the standardization of work to improve efficiency.
3 *Professional bureaucracy*, for example universities and hospitals, where the most important group is the operating core consisting of professional staff.

4 *Divisionalized form,* in many large multinational companies, where the middle line carries out the business with
top management taking the major investment decisions.
5 *Adhocracy,* as in special project groups in a highly complex
and unstable environment, such as NASA, the American
space agency, where the operating core and the support
staff work together by mutual adjustment.

Such typologies are of more interest to academics than
to managers, though it can be useful for a manager who is
moving from one type of organization to another to be able
to recognize what is different and hence what are the personal implications of working there. For example, a manager
who moves to a hospital from the armed services has to
adjust to the high autonomy exercised by professional staff
in a professional bureaucracy. Similarly some managers will
find it very hard to move from what Pugh and Hickson call
a full bureaucracy to one that is decentralized and has little
structure to its activities, what they call a 'non-bureaucracy'.
How difficult the adjustment will be depends partly upon
temperament, as some people prefer structure and authority
and feel very uncomfortable without them. A move in the other
direction from an informal kind of organization to a very
bureaucratic one may be even more traumatic!
    R. J. Butler's typology of the performance norms that are
appropriate for different industries is relevant to the regulators introduced for privatized industries.[14] It is also helpful
when thinking about the value of league tables. There are
two key dimensions: one is uniqueness versus comparability;
the other is clarity versus ambiguity. The regulator's task, or
that of the compiler of league tables, is easy where there are
plenty of similar organizations with which to compare and
where the bases of comparison are unambiguous. Combining
the two dimensions gives four types of organization:

1 Clear performance standards and comparable organizations, as in most businesses, when economic norms can
be applied.
2 Clear performance standards and non-comparable organizations, such as a government agency, when regulators tend
to set targets but cannot judge whether they are realistic.

3 Ambiguous performance standards but comparable organizations, when there is a lot of self-regulation as in
professional organizations.
4 Ambiguous performance standards and non-comparable
organizations, which is the most difficult, when moral
norms tend to be applied as in religious organizations,
charities or voluntary organizations. Regulation then is
based on trust, so it becomes especially important to
appoint highly trustworthy people to run the organization;
hence the sense of letdown when top people in a church
or charity are found to be stealing or using their position
to sexual advantage.

These different examples of typologies show the possible
benefits and the limitations of such classifications. The benefits are that the research has helped to identify what are the
key variables for distinguishing between organizations. Then it
is possible to go on as Burns and Stalker did to describe the
implications for working in these different types of organizations. The limitations are that any classification is limited; if it
is a short, easily understood one, it will necessarily be crude.

Both the Pugh and Hickson's and the Butler's typologies
are examples of the two-axis diagram with four quadrants,
which any manager who has been to lectures by social scientists will know is a favourite tool. There is the pleasure of
thinking up a name for each of the four quadrants. If you
don't like the academics' choice you can think what would
be better, or have a go at your own comparisons. A possibility is illustrated in Figure 6.1, from the author's earlier
work, of comparing two dimensions for judging how much
the manager needs to supervise immediate staff. One dimension is whether subordinates can do the job without the
manager's help; the other is whether they will do it. If the
immediate staff both know how to do their jobs and are well
motivated, then the manager has little supervision to do.

Summary

In this chapter we examined the problems that face managers
in designing a new organization or modifying an old one; and

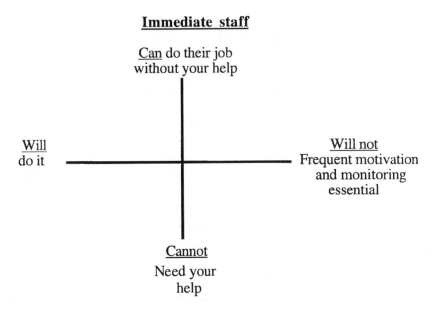

Immediate staff

Can do their job
without your help

Will
do it

Will not
Frequent motivation
and monitoring
essential

Cannot
Need your
help

Figure 6.1 Influencing needs in the job

considered the help they might get from social scientists' studies of organizational structures. We outlined the different decisions that have to be made in planning an organization. First is the division of work, where one of the major choices today is between what work is to be done within the organization and what by contract with other firms or individuals. Second is the basis to be used in grouping jobs together. Third is the question of how many levels of authority there should be. Management has to decide whether it wants to limit these to the smallest number possible. The general trend has been to cut the number of tiers in the organization. For the fourth we looked at the usefulness of organization charts and decided that they could be a useful tool, but one that is often abused. The limitations of such charts were stressed. The fifth is one of the most difficult decisions in planning an organization: how much decentralization there should be. This varies at different periods in the organization's history, depending in part on the extent to which common policies exist or are desired. The calibre of junior and middle management and the type of decisions to be made were among the other factors that affect how much decentralization there should be. In the sixth we examined the arguments for and against job descriptions. Their use depends both upon management philosophy and upon the rapidity of change.

Social scientists since the 1950s have studied organizational structures. Some of their findings are of direct relevance for managers. One of the most important from the early studies is that there is no one ideal form of organization, hence no universally applicable set of principles for its design. Instead the organization must be designed in accordance with its needs as these are determined by the environment within which it works. A few social scientists have been interested over the years in distinguishing different types of organization. Such studies are of more interest to academics than to managers but they have potential value for managers. They can help them to understand the particular characteristics of their own organization, why it is like that and why it is, or should be, changing. When moving to a different kind of organization, these typologies can help in recognizing how it is different and hence what adjustments they are likely to have to make.

7   People and organization

So far we have discussed the organization without the people who will bring it to life, make it work, and give it its distinctive character. Now we need to look at how people may influence the formal structure, as well as how the latter may affect people's behaviour by the demands it makes on them and the strains it imposes. First, let us look at an organization as seen through the eyes of a newly recruited manager and then more broadly at the social relations within an organization.

Learning the ropes

Managers joining a new company would soon make a gaffe if they relied upon the formal organization as their only guide to how the organization worked. The organization chart may embody management's intentions, but this planned structure is run by people and they will have an effect on how it works in practice. The formal organization does not, and cannot, show all the relationships that grow up between people; though in static conditions it will be more likely to do so than in periods of rapid change. An understanding of how the organization actually works is more necessary for the managers than a knowledge of the formal structure. Hence managers who move from one firm to another and, to a lesser extent, even from one department to another, will need time to learn how people work together. Only then will they know the best way to achieve what they want. They must find out, if they are to work effectively and to get on, how the status order differs from that shown on the chart; who takes the lead, and in what circumstances, and who follows. They must also be sensitive to the power politics, to whether management is divided into cliques and, if so, how the cliques are made up and what their relation is to each other. Then they

will need to know whom they must get on their side if they
wish to sell an idea. In one company it will usually be sufficient to get the support of the managing director. In another,
staff as well as colleagues may need to be in agreement.
There may be one or two influential people, not necessarily
the most senior, whose opinion can sway the others.

The ways of finding out what is happening in a company
will also vary. In some there may be committees and informal
meetings for the exchange of information; in others the
canteen may be the best source of news. In most companies
there will be one or more people who are particularly well-
informed about what is happening – 'Ask old Bill, he will
know.' On the shop floor the best place for information may
be the lavatory – a useful source for the social research
worker but of no use to the manager, who will usually be
closeted in a separate place. Women managers can be at a
disadvantage. In many firms one finds attractive new wash-
rooms to provide for the advent of women in previously
all-male managements. The women gain in privacy but lose
in the opportunities for informal talk.

New managers have to learn the do's and don'ts, the
unwritten rules, which may well be different from those in
their previous organization. They must learn when they can
write or ring and when they must go and see the person if
they want information. In some companies, acceptance by
colleagues may partly depend on conversation at lunchtime,
and they should know what topics are taboo. Dress may still
be subject to some important don'ts – in one company when
a man asked why he did not get an annual salary increase,
he was told that it was because he had worn a sweater
instead of a jacket, which 'showed that he was obviously not
taking his management position seriously'. The ambitious
manager will want to know what are the standards of 'taking
one's job seriously'. In this example dress was important;
elsewhere it may be getting to one's desk early or staying
late. But in a few – all too few – companies, habitual over-
time may be judged a sign of inefficiency. All these informal
customs and procedures will help to give an organization its
character, will make it different from another company that
has the same formal structure. These the new managers must
learn before they can become effective members of the

management team. They will benefit from a general understanding of how people work together in an organization, but
they will also need the detailed knowledge of how their particular organization works, if they are to make it work to their
advantage.

How people work together

When people work together, they establish social relationships and customary ways of doing things. This can be called
the informal organization, that is, the patterns of behaviour
that get established. It is not the behaviour that is described
in any organization manual or suggested by any organization chart. How people work together in practice cannot be
laid down in even the most comprehensive job descriptions,
as it will depend, at least in part, upon the relations that
develop between people – hence, on the kind of people they
are, their particular strengths and weaknesses and how they
react to each other. Therefore, an organization is not just a
collection of isolated individuals performing the specific functions of their allotted jobs. It is also a set of social relations
made up of how A reacts to B and both of them to C, of
social groups that influence the attitudes and actions of their
members and, sometimes, also of a number of cliques or
factions – groups that are organized against others. Two
things tend to happen when people work together: they may
form social groups and they may develop informal methods
of getting their work done, that is, informal organization. Both
of these can have important effects on efficiency.

When several people work in close contact with each other
for any length of time, they are likely to become a social
group. They are then more than a collection of individuals
who happen to be working together, and acquire a sense of
identity as a group in which some people are inside and
others outside. There may be several social groups within
one large work group and some individuals who do not belong
to a group. The social group will have a sense of like-mind-
edness among its members and will agree on many subjects
of immediate importance to them. What they agree on will
depend upon the purposes the group serves.

The cohesiveness that members of a social group develop can have great strengths. The social support that comes from a close-knit group can be exciting and encourage what would otherwise seem a superhuman effort. It brings dangers too: 'we belong, others are outsiders'. This can be the basis for fruitful competition, fruitful in that all try harder to do well and to win, but it can also lead to antagonism and to lack of cooperation. Hence managers need to be aware of the power and the dangers of social groups. Good managers provide the climate in which groups want to pursue aims that match their own. Good managers, too, organize work so that those who need to cooperate with each other have opportunities to become friendly rather than to see each other as the enemy.

This tendency for people who work together to develop social groups has important implications for management, as it can materially assist or considerably handicap management objectives. A number of studies have shown that enthusiasm for work is much greater where group affiliations have been built up, provided the aims of the group do not run counter to those of management. People enjoy their work more, and are less likely to be absent from work, because they have become part of a social group in which they are important as a person.

Informal groups within the formal organization can also work against management aims. They will have their own aims, which may support or oppose management aims. They will also have their own sanctions, which will differ from those in the formal organization: these will consist of the withdrawal of acceptance and help by the group. The degree to which this is done will depend upon the heinousness of the infringement of the group's aims. In extreme cases the individual may be ostracized. When the informal group is strong, its sanctions are likely to be more compelling on a group member than those of management, since they are more certain to be applied. Management may not catch a culprit who is violating one of the official rules, but the informal group is much more likely to know if one of its members breaks its social code.

One of the greatest advantages of a group is to facilitate coordination. Its self-disciplining and self-checking means that far less management time and effort are necessary to ensure that work is being carried out satisfactorily. But this is only valuable where the group is working to further management aims. Whether the informal group will work with or against management aims will depend upon whether or not management has gained the staff's commitment. This is such an important subject for any manager that it was discussed in Chapter 3, 'Getting the job done'.

All organizations develop informal methods for getting work done, and these may facilitate or oppose management aims. The importance of informal organization has long been recognized. Chester Barnard, an American executive writing in the 1930s, said that its functions at the management level are:

> ... raising issues calling for decisions, without dissipating dignity and objective authority and without overloading executive positions; also to minimize excessive cliques of political types arising from too great divergence of interest and views; to promote self-discipline of the group; and to make possible the development of important personal influences in the organization.[1]

Hence informal organization can serve to sift information and ideas before they go to formal authority. Some things, too, can be done informally, often with the knowledge and agreement of senior management, which it would be embarrassing to acknowledge as official policy. However, with the greater emphasis on corporate probity this should happen less than before.

We so often take informal organization for granted that we tend to talk as if it did not exist. Many top managers when asked about the organization of their company would describe the formal organization without adding any reservations about the way it operates in practice. A description of how top management worked in a medium-sized company will illustrate some of the differences between the formal and informal organization. The organization chart in Figure 7.1 puts all the senior managers who reported to the managing director on the same level. Preliminary inquiries soon showed that the top group were not, as the chart implied, of equal importance. The sales manager was really only a junior office manager, since the managing director took a strong personal interest in sales and in effect acted as the sales manager,

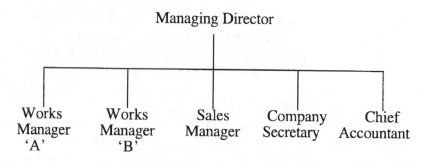

Figure 7.1 An organization chart of senior managers in a medium-sized company

playing an active part in the day-to-day running of the department. It would not take much time to discover the actual status and responsibility of the sales manager, but it would probably need some experience of how this top management worked in practice to find out that one of these senior managers, the chief accountant, was the most important. He was frequently consulted by the managing director on many aspects of the business and was also used by his colleagues, because his advice carried weight with the managing director, to interpret their grievances or ideas to him. The actual role of the chief accountant could not have been guessed at by looking at the organization chart. A more realistic picture of status and communication in this company is shown in Figure 7.2. The dotted lines show the second channel for communication. The chief accountant is not put in a direct line between the managing director and the other top managers, as he does not function, either officially or unofficially, as the assistant managing director but merely as adviser and interpreter.

Chester Barnard, discussing a role similar to that of the chief accountant, suggested that:

> ... many men not only exercise beneficent influence far beyond that implied by their formal status, but most of them, at the time, would lose their influence if they had corresponding formal status. The reason may be that men may have personal qualifications of high order that will not operate under the stress of commensurate official responsibility.[2]

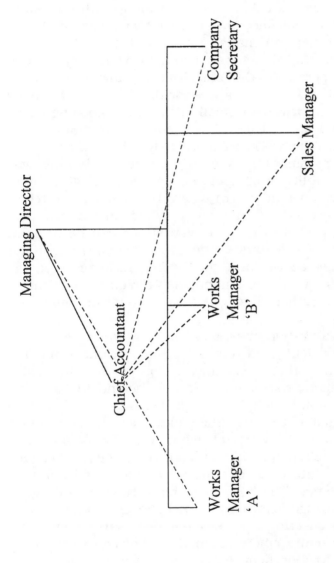

Figure 7.2 A more realistic version of Figure 7.1 for that particular company

Such a manager can help to reduce the isolation of the chief executive by acting as a trusted go-between who carries messages to and from the heights. In the example given above, top management worked more efficiently because the role played by the chief accountant helped to offset the managing director's weaknesses in dealing with his staff. The success of the chief accountant's role was, however, based on trust; the other top managers found that it was easier to get the managing director to listen to what they wanted if they could persuade the chief accountant to sell their ideas or to explain their grievances for them, and they trusted him to put them forward in good faith. The managing director also trusted the advice of the chief accountant. Such a relation can only work harmoniously where there is an absence of personal animosity. (In our example this was helped by the futility of competition for the managing director's post. It was a family firm where the managing director would be succeeded by his son.) Where there are personality clashes, cliques may develop which can be harmful to efficiency. If, for instance, the other managers had not trusted the chief accountant, they would have resented his close relations with the managing director and might have banded together and given him only the minimum cooperation.

Informal organization may also develop to bypass or to protect an inefficient individual or group. In one company, for instance, as other departments found that the sales control department was inaccurate and behind in its work, they gradually took to doing the work themselves, but routing the final estimates through the sales department. Senior management was unaware of what was happening and nobody would tell them for fear of getting their colleagues in sales control into trouble. In this example, good relations masked inefficiency. This may often happen when colleagues seek to cover up the slowness or inefficiency of one of their number. Such 'covering up' need not necessarily stem from antagonism to management. Sometimes, of course, it does, especially on the shop floor. Even with improved information technology, opportunities for covering up may still be found.

Informal organization may also develop because rapid change makes the formal organization out-of-date. Initially, in changing conditions people will try to solve problems on an *ad hoc* basis as they arise but, sooner or later, if the formal organization is not adapted to meet the new situation, they will develop informal ways of coping. If, for instance, interdepartmental meetings are not set up to keep people in the picture, or fail to do so, managers from different departments may make a habit of dropping in to a local pub once or twice a week to try as one manager put it, 'to sort out the chaos'. The tendency of people to develop informal methods of coping with change has probably saved many companies that have failed to adapt their formal structure to radical changes in their environment.

How the organization affects people

People may modify the formal organization, but it is a reciprocal influence, for the way work is organized also affects the behaviour of individuals and groups. It can impose pressures on people in particular jobs that may lead them to adopt informal means of trying to avoid, or lessen, the problems of their position. The influence of the organization of work on the behaviour of individuals is most clearly seen when people in the same jobs in different parts of the organization are found to react in similar ways. A fifty-year-old study by Ralph H. Turner,[3] of the disbursement officer in the American Navy (supply officer), still provides a good illustration of organizational pressures on particular jobholders and of how people may react to them. Similar examples can be found today in other organizations – but it is not the kind of research that gains academic credits today as attention has shifted to other subjects, like the effects of organizational culture on people's behaviour.

Turner found that the particular problems of the disbursement officer's job were: one, possible conflicts between regulations governing his function and orders from his superior, both of which were supposed to be obeyed; two, the fact that he held a lower rank than that of many of his clients; and three, pressure from people with whom he was in close contact and who wanted him to interpret the regulations in their favour. The last was made more difficult by a well-developed informal system for the exchange of favours, so that it was often hard for a man to get the services and equipment essential for his job, quite apart from personal goods, unless he could promise some return. If the disbursement officer stuck to the strictly formal procedure, he lost his potentially strong position in the system of mutual benefits. According to Ralph Turner:

> Two general tendencies emerge among disbursing officers as the consequences of orders conflicting with regulations and the pressures of rank and informal structure. One is differential treatment of clientele. Because of the time consumed in extra routine treatment of persons on the 'in', others get summary treatment. The second tendency is for loop-holes in regulations to become tools in the hand of the disbursing officer to elevate his own status. Thus he may become more concerned with his own bargaining power than with correct application of the rules.[4]

An example of one occupational group being viewed with suspicion by others is provided by a study of management accountants. In this study one manager said:

> The accounting system is geared to meet the needs of the board. It's a control instrument ... my needs are different ... I need the information for management ... but it's too imperfect ... but the board get it so we must be ready with answers to questions on variances.[5]

This manager illustrated the defensive reactions that accounting procedures can arouse. In one department studied the distrust of the accountants and their figures was so great that managers ran their own accounting system to provide information for decisions and to challenge the information provided by the accountants.

These, and other studies, show that many reactions that are put down to individual cussedness are due to pressures imposed by the situation in which the person has to work: pressures that are likely to produce a similar reaction in people of very different personalities. These are important findings, for they show that managers need to think more of the strains that may result from the form of organization.

Problems are usually discussed in terms of personality, but the remedy may be to change the organization rather than the people. Several studies also show that the nature of the technological organization can have important effects on social relations in the working group. It can determine the amount and type of social contact that people can have with one another, hence the likelihood of social groups and satisfying relations developing.

The classic study by Walker and Guest of assembly line workers in a car factory showed that the technological layout and the high noise level imposed considerable restrictions on the amount of contact workers could have with one another. It also largely determined the amount and type of contact they had with supervision.[6] One study by the Tavistock Institute of Human Relations of different methods of coal-getting showed that a change in the method had radically altered the kind of social relations that had developed in association with the old method.[7] In another of the Institute's studies of the coal industry,[8] the research workers found striking differences between output, costs and absenteeism for two methods of work organization. For instance, the absenteeism rate from all causes was 20 per cent of possible shifts under one method and 8.2 per cent under another. Both studies suggest that the method of work organization prevented the worker from establishing satisfactory social relations, which is likely to be bad for morale and may show itself in high absenteeism.

The growing awareness of the bad effects of assembly line production on the workers led to the interest in job design to make for the human use of human beings and so to motivate people to work well. This is a subject that has been heavily researched, particularly in the USA. Hackman and Oldham,[9] two of the main researchers in this area, concluded that what was needed was:

1 Work that the individual saw to be meaningful.
2 Responsibility for the outcomes.
3 Knowledge of the results.

They described what work characteristics would contribute to the first:

1 A variety of different activities that provide some challenge by involving the use of different skills and talents.
2 Doing a job from start to finish with a visible outcome.
3 The job affects other people's welfare.

The more autonomy the job provides in scheduling the work and determining the procedures to be used, the greater will be the feeling of responsibility for the outcome.

Hackman and Oldham's theories have been supported by subsequent research, but have also been criticized for too narrow a focus, such as not including the interpersonal aspects of the job. The focus of all the earlier work on job redesign was on jobs where the jobholders work relatively independently of each other.[10] The growing use of work teams with considerable autonomy introduces new types of jobs. Studies of the effects of such teams on productivity, atten-dandance and group member satisfaction have been very positive. Cotton, reviewing the literature, found that self-directed work teams increased productivity in 83 per cent of the studies, decreased absenteeism in 79 per cent and increased job satisfaction in 93 per cent.[11] This suggests that this new approach to work organization can do much to improve how people feel about their work and their commit-ment to it.

The many changes that have been taking place in organi-zations are a source of work pressure today. Two surveys can tell us how common are feelings of work stress. One was a random national sample of 3,855 in Britain in 1992 of those in work aged between twenty and sixty. The res-ponse rate was 72 per cent. This study also asked about job satisfaction. The results showed that jobs were found to be more satisfying than before, which was attributed to more jobs in the service sector and jobs requiring more skill. There was little difference in the level of satisfaction and the level of the job, with skilled manual workers being the least satisfied. The main influence on satisfaction was whether they had an increase in their skills over the last five years.

The price of these changes in jobs, the survey shows, has been a sharp increase in pressures at work. Over half the respondents said that the stress in their jobs had increased in the last five years and only 12 per cent thought that it had decreased. People are working harder and have more responsibility for their work and quality standards. This has made work more demanding and more stressful. Respondents were asked four questions about how they felt at the end of the day, for example: 'I feel used up at the end of a workday' and 'After I leave work I keep worrying about work problems'. They were asked to rate their answers from 'all of the time' to 'never'. On the basis of these answers 31 per cent of employees regularly experienced a high level of stress. The stress level was highest among professional and managerial workers at 39 per cent.[12]

A study of mental health among NHS staff in 19 NHS trusts showed that they suffered more from stress than workers generally. One indication of this is the higher incidence of sickness amongst NHS staff. Another is the number reporting minor psychiatric problems serious enough to benefit from professional help: 27 per cent of male managers and 41 per cent of women. A variety of explanations have been given, such as management cutbacks, the nature of the work, and autocratic management. The differences between trusts, and the changes made in individual trusts, show that good management can do much to reduce stress levels. The provision of health promotion campaigns, occupational health service and a staff counselling service are all thought to have helped one trust to reduce sickness absences substantially.[13]

In recent years attention has shifted from the effects of the organization of work on people's behaviour to how behaviour is influenced by the organizational culture. What is much more common today is the widespread recognition that organizational change is not just, or even necessarily mainly, about changing the structure but often requires changing the culture too. Much management training for managers from the same organization is aimed at doing that. Many managers today would recognize that organizations have a distinctive culture and could describe some of the characteristics of the culture in their own organization. They may also describe which of these characteristics they think need changing if the organization is to cope well with the changes taking place.

Whistle-blowing

The social pressures on individuals in organizations make it very hard for anyone to blow the whistle. A group of bank managers discussing what a subordinate should do if he found his branch manager was fiddling the books agreed that if he did report it to a more senior manager it would harm his career, because he would be seen as someone who told tales. Similarly doctors tend to cover up the deficiencies of colleagues even though these can be harmful to patient care. The position of the whistle-blower is a hard one because he or she will be regarded by colleagues as lacking in loyalty and even superiors are likely to be distrustful of the whistle-blower. Studies both in the USA and the UK confirm that whistle-blowing is almost always costly to the individual, resulting in career disruption and personal abuse.[14] Yet such employees can be very valuable, so organizations need to adopt a code of practice for whistle-blowing.

It can be just as difficult to try to warn that plans are failing, as Lee Roy Beach explains:

> Implementation of a plan mobilizes many people and lots of resources; it is difficult for anyone to stand up and proclaim that it is failing. Even worse, it is difficult to appear to be the 'quitter', the person who is ready to admit defeat. Courage is often confused with persistence, and few of us want to admit a lack of courage. The result may be that even when cracks begin to appear and things start to go wrong, plans stay in place because no one wants to be the one who blows the whistle. Given these pressures, organizations often find it nearly impossible to provide social support for being honest. ... Asking subordinates for honesty is often the same as asking them to forfeit their careers.[15]

Summary

The structure of an organization is modified by the people who work in it, so that even otherwise identical organizations will develop their own distinctive characters. People will develop their own ways of working together, which is called the 'informal organization'. This can be a great asset, as it can make allowances for personalities, adapt to change and facilitate coordination. The social groups that tend to develop among those working closely together may be an important factor in promoting good morale, because people will then find their work more socially satisfying. Social groups may also work against management aims: morale may be high, but because of the common cause of defeating management's objectives.

The relation between the formal organization and people is a reciprocal one. People modify the working of the formal organization, but their behaviour is also influenced by it. It may make demands on them which they find an undue strain, so that they seek ways of modifying these pressures. The method of work organization can determine how people relate to one another, which may affect both their productivity and their morale. Managers, therefore, need to be conscious of the ways in which methods of work organization may influence people's attitudes and actions. Before behaviour is put down to individual or group cussedness, managers should look for its possible organizational causes.

Concerns today about the effects on people of the organization of work are very different from those shown in the early studies. The focus is no longer on the boring, repetitive and socially constraining nature of many factory jobs. Many of the jobs today are different, they are less boring and impose fewer restrictions on social contact. But the price for more challenging jobs is an increase in stress. More jobs are now worrying rather than boring.

Social pressures can make it too career threatening to blow the whistle when something is wrong. Even senior management may be suspicious of the whistle-blower.

Part Three **Contrasts in Management**

In Part Three we shall look at some of the contrasts in the manager's job. We shall see how greatly it varies according to the situation of the company and the prevailing codes of behaviour. The first chapter describes how the time and the place affect the ways in which a manager thinks and acts. A Japanese, Indian, French or German manager will often take different decisions from a British manager in the same position. The British manager today will manage differently from his/her predecessor of a hundred years ago. The second chapter discusses some of the problems inherent in managing a large organization. The third chapter looks at the ways in which rapid change can revolutionize the nature of the manager's job, and at how to manage change.

8 The social environment of management

Many management textbooks are written in abstract terms about what managers do and how they do it, but few are concerned with what managers do in real life, still less with why they do it. Once one begins to look at the 'why' of managers' actions, one finds that many of them are influenced by their particular environment. This is true both of the way in which managers behave to other people and of the type of business decisions that they take. How they treat their employees, each other, their directors and their customers, will partly depend on their character, but still more on what is customary at the time in their company, industry, locality and country. Whether they seek to expand their business rapidly, to undercut their competitors, to misrepresent their products, or to put customer satisfaction before economic production will again, at least partly, depend on the prevailing mores. The culture, both of the country and the organization, comprises all the social factors that affect the way people behave. In this chapter we discuss some of those social factors.

National differences

What managers strive for, and the rules they observe in doing so, will be influenced, and often determined, by the accepted goals and mores of their society. All management in private enterprise must be interested in profits, if they are to survive in normal circumstances. The importance they attach to them and how they seek to achieve them will vary in different societies and at different stages in the same society. Economic goals, such as maximum profits, an expanding share of the market, greater productivity and lower costs, may be modified by social goals, such as offering an assured livelihood to long-term employees, even if this means retaining the inefficient, or not causing economic hardship by forcing one's competitor out of business.

In a rapidly industrializing society, entrepreneurs and managers are the path-makers who will change or destroy many of the old ways of life. Yet the extent to which business determines the goals of a society varies greatly from one industrial country to another. Perhaps only in America could the head of a nation have said, 'The Business of America is Business'.[1] In terms of a country's livelihood this is truer of the UK, but business is still not the core of British society, nor are business men and women the major influence in setting the society's goals. One test of whether business mores dominate society might be whether the explanation of an action as 'good business' is considered more acceptable in the USA than in the UK and more acceptable in the UK than in France. Many common business practices in the UK, such as attempts to mislead the consumer into thinking that the size of the pack shows how much it contains or a guarantee more valuable than it is, would be called dishonest by the man in the street.

The status of American managers is higher than that of their European counterparts. This has important repercussions, both on recruitment and on the attitudes of top managers. In societies where social prestige is determined by social origins and occupation rather than by one's standard of living, the drawing power of industry's high rewards will be less. British business as a career has suffered, until recently, from the greater prestige of the civil service and the professions, but now business, or at least big business, is becoming more respectable. If successful business men and women have a high status in their society, they will probably be content to devote their energies to business. In a society like the British, where greater prestige still attaches to other occupations, the ambitious and successfully businessman who wants a title was likely to devote an increasing amount of time to public activities. This may have been good for society but it diluted the drive to improve the business. Now it is possible to get a title for services to business, thus recognizing the contribution that it makes to the country.

The extent of competition between companies and between individuals varies considerably from one country to another. In part this is a result of external pressures. In the USA companies are often forced by anti-trust laws to be more competitive than they would choose. In part the amount of competition depends upon business mores and the ruthlessness with which a company will seek to expand its share of the market. The internationalization of many companies, with cross-border takeovers, mergers and alliances, has reduced but by no means eliminated the importance of national differences.

The amount of competition between individuals and the degree to which inefficiency is tolerated are also strongly influenced by the kind of society in which industry grows up. Competition between individuals is stronger in the USA than in Britain. In the USA the inefficient manager will be fired more readily than in Britain. In the latter, incompetent but long-service managers in a large company used to be kicked upstairs and given jobs with a high-sounding title but which did not let them handicap the firm's efficiency. From the 1970s on, greater competitive pressures meant a harsher approach was taken, though if old enough they may have been given generous terms for early retirement. Then their livelihood and their feelings would have been spared. In Japan, where the preservation of individual status and prestige is much more important than with us, this practice is the customary one.

Many more companies and managers in other kinds of organizations are having to learn to work with managers from other countries. Hence it is important to know what is different about the way they see their job and how this may affect their behaviour. It is easy to anticipate that Japanese, Chinese, Indian, African and Arab managers will have a different approach, but the considerable differences that exist in other Western cultures also need to be understood. One of the differences between British and German managers, for example, is that British managers make a much less clear-cut separation between work and private life. German managers emphasize punctuality, work hard and leave on time. British managers take a more social view of work which means that they may gossip with colleagues, have a drink with them but may also stay late or, if the operation is on shift-working, drop in at the weekend to see how things are going. German managers attach more importance to following procedures rigorously and see the British as undisciplined, whereas the British may see them as inflexible and lacking initiative. The German managers will be better qualified than the British and middle managers will have stayed longer in their present jobs. Both of which give them a more in-depth knowledge of the operations.[2]

French managers differ from British managers in other ways. Their educational credentials will be far more important than for British managers in determining their career. When at work relations will be much more formal so that the individual does not have to become so personally involved. The existence of two forms of address 'tu' for informal and 'vous' for formal and respectful give scope, that does not exist in Britain, for making social distinctions. 'Vous' is the norm in business so that any use of 'tu' is marked, sometimes as a way of showing that one belongs to the same clique.[3] French managers talk to each other much less than British and American managers, according to a study of the behaviour of managers on courses at INSEAD. They also developed fewer relationships with managers from other countries: the Americans and Canadians did so more than the other nationalities.[4]

A study of the behaviour of managers on courses at INSEAD found that British and American managers talked with other managers ten times more than the French managers.

Nor are France and Germany the only European countries to have management differences from the British. Distinctive characteristics can be found in the other countries, too, though compared with Japan, all share some similarities. Chief among them is a more individualist approach.

Lessons from abroad

In Britain continuing concern about its relatively low productivity has led to the search for useful lessons from abroad.

A major attempt was made after the Second World War to find out what lessons the USA could teach British industry. British teams of managers, trade unionists and technicians visited the same industries in the USA, under the auspices of the Anglo-American Productivity Council. They enthused about the atmosphere of American business: the great optimism, cost consciousness and continual search for improved methods.[5] Americans at all levels are, they reported, more productivity-minded. Previous foreign observers had said the same thing. British visitors to the USA still notice a difference today, even if it is not as great as before.

The British productivity teams, impressed by the greater American concern for productivity, sought for explanations of this difference in attitude. They found them in the greater social and geographic mobility of American society; the higher status of the businessman and the greater support given to the making of profits and the accumulation of capital; the greater competitiveness, both between companies and individuals; and the more practical, technical orientation of American education. They also pointed to the widespread desire for a higher standard of living and the part played in this by the American woman who acted as the pacemaker in striving for a higher standard of living: '... viewed from the standpoint of high national industrial productivity, the influence, in this way of the American woman must be regarded as distinctly valuable.[6]

Thirty-five years later another British team reported on their visit to the USA to study 'New technology: Manpower aspects of the management of change'. They came from the heavy electrical machinery industry. Like their predecessors they thought that there was a more positive attitude to improvement in the American firms that they visited. Talking about the introduction of new technology in their industry, particularly programmable automation, they said:

> ... that commitment was seen as only the beginning of a series of complex managerial decisions and organizational and motivational adjustments within the company. These changes might more easily be made by North American than by UK companies.[7]

Concern about the productivity of British industry has continued. In 1993 an article in *The Sunday Times* claimed that a secret report from the Department of Trade and Industry had found that British industry had inferior management, inadequate investment in new technology and with productivity levels at least 25 per cent below its international competitors such as Germany and France.[8]

The United States used to be the mecca for those seeking to improve their productivity and cost effectiveness, but strong competition from South East Asia has changed this. Now Japan and more recently other rapidly developing South East Asian countries are seen as even more impressively successful. The Americans have been interested since the 1970s to discover the reasons for Japanese success, especially in automobiles and electronics. The fear was that the explanation lay in Japanese culture, so that there would be no lessons applicable in the West. Fortunately the establishment of Japanese subsidiaries abroad provided an opportunity to study how they managed the locals. This showed that in the USA and in Britain the Japanese could manage successfully plants that had been ailing under local management. So the Japanese firms established in Britain have brought not only employment and money but also, unexpectedly, lessons in how to manage! Many Japanese methods have now been adopted successfully by American and British companies, though sometimes the idea came from the USA originally, as with total quality management, but was only taken seriously by the Japanese.

In Britain a study by Michael White and Malcolm Trevor in the early 1980s of the experience of British workers managed by Japanese produced useful if rather shaming lessons for British managers. They found that the British workers in Japanese manufacturing companies that they studied liked working for Japanese managers and regretted their departure. They liked their greater involvement in production and their more egalitarian approach, compared with British managers. The authors contrasted the human relations approach originating in the USA, with its emphasis on the need for managers to be people-centred as well as task-centred, with the Japanese approach, saying:

... Leadership and motivation are subjects which Japanese managers whom we met in Britain hardly talked about. It is true that they set much store by the recruitment of 'good workers', and they took pride in the quality of their work-force. But they seemed to assume that workers would be well motivated. Moreover, to a most striking and extreme degree, they were task-centred in their management style and practices ... the single-minded Japanese emphasis on the task seems to find a ready acceptance among British workers.[9]

They concluded that:

One implication is that motivation and leadership are much less a matter of the individual manager's approach and much more a matter of the whole system of working.[10]

A comparative study of British and German middle managers in comparable companies in the early 1990s found that the Germans, like the Japanese, were very task-oriented and more egalitarian than the British. The task orientation may be explained in part by their background which was more specialized than their British counterparts and in part by their view of the job. The British managers stressed delegation and people management whereas the Germans were much more involved in the actual work and saw themselves as a technical resource for their staff.[11] They were more interested in the product than the British managers who saw themselves primarily as managers. A possible conclusion from these comparisons with Japanese and German managers is that in Britain, and in America too, being a manager has been overemphasized and that a greater focus on the product itself, whether manufactured or a service, would improve the firm's efficiency.

The background of management

What managers think and how they behave are partly determined by their environment, the country, the stage of industrialization, the locality, and the industry. They are also influenced by their own background, which is in itself a product of their environment. The social and educational background of managers, and the experience they obtain, will depend upon a variety of social and historical facts, such as how industry started in their country, the stage of industrialization, the status of industry in society, the importance attached to different occupations, the educational system and the nature and strength of the barriers to occupational mobility.

The backgrounds of the early owners and managers differed from one country to another. Where the family played an important part in the growth of business and still holds many of the top jobs, this may make for conservatism. But family management is not necessarily conservative, as the history of some of the British and German industrial families shows. In many countries family connections are important for getting into management posts. Hence, the power of the family in business can largely prevent management or, at least, top management from being a career open to the talents. In most countries family management has been largely replaced by professional management, though the extent to which this is true varies for historical and taxation reasons.

The professional background of top managers is likely to affect their judgement of what is important: hence company policy. In those countries, like Germany, where engineers predominate, they will probably emphasize production and pay less attention to marketing. Where, as in many large British companies, accountants play an important part in top management, they may be chiefly concerned with the financial standing of the firm, since this affects the ease with which the company can raise capital. The proportion of university graduates among the managers may also affect the attitude to management. The UK is noteworthy among Western countries for having an unusually small proportion of graduates in management.

Where graduates are recruited, the jobs they will be able to do will be restricted by the strength of local traditions and the extent to which graduates and workers share a common background. It is more common for graduates to work in junior production and service jobs in American than in British companies. This is partly due to the greater number of college graduates in the USA, and partly to the greater possibility of graduates and workers being able to talk the same language. The American graduate is more likely to have gone to the same school and to have spent university vacations working as an operative.

As industry becomes larger and more complex, the demands on management become greater. Hence, with increasing industrialization, the background of managers tends to change. Professional management, selected and promoted on merit, takes the place of managers chosen by nepotism and the 'old boy' network. This is only true in countries where the class barriers are sufficiently fluid to permit it. Studies in the USA and the UK in the 1950s showed that merit was by no means the only qualification for getting to the top. A study by the Acton Trust Society of the background of over 3,000 British managers in industry showed that a man who had been to a public school had ten times the average chance of becoming a manager – none were women.[12] Comparisons with a study of managers' backgrounds in the USA suggested that the proportion of top managers who came up from the bottom in Britain was 15 per cent and in the USA 20 per cent.[13] 'Up from the bottom' was defined as their having no special educational qualifications, and starting their career as labourers, clerks or salesmen.

A large-scale study of British managers in the early 1980s analysed the father's occupation for 1,058 members of the British Institute of Management and concluded that:

> ... a majority of managers came from middle class origins (irrespective of the definition of middle class employed); only just over a quarter originated from the highest echelons of the socio-economic structure as measured by the Registrar General's Class 1 grading. Thus, while modern managers are clearly disproportionately recruited from the upper strata of society, the pattern reveals that origins are not typically exclusive and in no way warrant any suggestion that they constitute a self-perpetuating elite. Indeed, nearly a third of the sample were nurtured in 'blue collar' homes, while the fathers of nearly 6 per cent were unskilled manual workers.[14]

It is not possible to say whether the social background of British managers had changed over the twenty-five years because the two samples are not comparable and the methods used for assessing social advantage are different. The later study is based on father's occupation at the height of his career and the former on education and starting job in the company. It is clear that it remained an advantage to have a higher social background if one is to become a manager: an advantage but not a prerequisite.

Concern about inequality has shifted from an emphasis on the social class background of managers, all or almost all men, in the early studies to a wider concern today for equality of opportunities for women and ethnic minorities. There have been major changes, especially in the number of women who are now managers. Yet, despite all the publicity, the declarations in employers' recruitment that they are an equal opportunity employer, women managers are still a small minority in many companies – the public sector has done better – and the number of women in top management posts is tiny. People from ethnic minorities have fared even less well than women. Women and even more people from ethnic minorities in the UK have found it easier to succeed by founding their own businesses than by trying to get to the top in established ones.

Management's attitude to labour

How managers regard their employees is reflected in management's attitude to authority, on the one hand, and the conditions of work and employee services, on the other. Management's attitude to labour has changed greatly in the last fifty years in Britain and the USA. It also differs considerably from one country to another, and even, to a lesser extent, from one industry or locality to another. Management may be authoritarian (expecting unquestioning obedience to orders and without concern for the employee's welfare); authoritarian and paternalistic; constitutional (acting in accordance with the rules laid down by government, trade unions, and management); or, at least to some extent, democratic (that is, permitting employees some share in decision-making).

How much authority management has and how it exercises it depend partly on the width of the gap that exists in class and education between management and workers, and partly on the limitations on management's freedom of action that are imposed by government and trade unions. Managers' authority generally declines with increasing industrialization. The standard of living rises and the length of education increases, making the background of managers and managed more alike, so that management's authority can rest less on social distance.[15] The change in the composition of the work-force, with many fewer jobs for unskilled workers and many more for technical and professional staff, has had the same effect.

The gap, or social distance, that exists between different levels in the organization reflects both the class structure in the society as a whole and management's place in it. In a very class-bound society much of management's authority may rest on social distance; whether it does so effectively will depend upon the relations existing between management and labour. In a country that still retains some feudal tradi-tions, management may receive the natural social deference that social inferiors give to their superiors. Where no feudal tradition remains, this type of authority is likely to be strongly resented.

Nowadays the part played by government in establishing rules for employee conditions is likely to be the greatest in the early stages of industrialism. Conditions in the older industrial countries set a standard by which employee treat-ment in the underdeveloped country can be judged, but the unions are not yet powerful enough to ensure adequate protection. So the workers turn to the government. In Latin America the government plays a very active role in industrial relations, partly because of the hesitations that workers, in a highly stratified society, experience in expressing their diffi-culties direct to management. In such a society there is a much stronger emphasis on authority and deference to the superior than in the English-speaking countries. The workers, therefore, find it easier to get somebody in a government labour department to express their grievances to manage-ment.

It should be remembered what a change there has been in Britain, as in other Western countries, in the employer's attitude to the employee. In the early days of industrializa-tion the large majority of British employers, who might otherwise have been kind-hearted men, had no feeling of responsibility for the welfare of their employees and were only forced by the Factory Acts to provide minimal conditions for health and safety. As Croome and Hammond pointed out:

> The new manufacturers, with a few honourable exceptions, felt no responsibility for the welfare of their workers; nor was their own self-interest enlightened enough to show them that better work can be got from well-paid, well-fed, well-housed men and women working under decent conditions for reasonable hours, than from half-starved, brutalized and exhausted workers and over-driven children. The treatment of children in the new factories was, indeed, the crowning disgrace of the Industrial Revolution. Hours in the cotton factories were anything up to sixteen a day and rarely below twelve. ... The workers were completely under the thumb of their 'masters and proprietors', to use the then Lord Londonderry's phrase, subject to arbitrary overtime, arbitrary punishment, arbitrary fines and deductions, and arbitrary dismissal.[16]

Even the differences in some companies between the 1930s and the present day are marked. What would be considered normal practice then would be considered inhuman today.

Once management accepts some responsibility for its employees, it may show this in several way. It may be paternalistic, either because this is, as in Japan, a carry-over from a feudal society, or because management chooses to express its concern for its employees' welfare in that way and meets little or no opposition from them to the dependent role implicit in paternalism. Paternalistic employers are still sometimes found in the USA and UK, although they are more common in countries like Italy, where class divisions are stronger.

Nor does paternalism necessarily vanish with advancing industrialism, for in Japan, a highly industrialized country, full-time employees can expect to stay with the company until they retire and to receive a great range of social benefits from the company. Flexibility is provided by part-time employees who do not have the same security. Whereas in bad times Western companies will make staff redundant, Japanese management will see it as their duty to increase demand or to find new products to use the company's resources. This much greater job security for Japanese full-time employees is one of the reasons why Japanese employees identify much more with their companies that do Western employees.

The amount of paternalism practised by employers in different countries will be affected by the extent to which the state provides welfare services. State provision makes the worker, and the manager, less dependent upon a paternalistic employer. Increasingly, good employee conditions in many countries are more of a right than a favour – a right that comes from legislation or from trade union agreements.

Paternalistic management is likely to take what Fox called a 'unitary' perspective.[17] So do many managers who work for companies where employee rights and conditions are negotiated. The 'unitary' view emphasizes the sense of togetherness, the achievement of common organizational goals and the legitimacy of management. Industrial relations problems are seen as either the fault of trade unions or as coming from poor communication and other managerial failings. The opposite perspective Fox called 'pluralist'. This view recognizes that any organization is made up of a variety of interest groups, with management and labour being the two principal ones. Trade unions represent the legitimate interest of labour, and differences with management should be resolved, where possible, by bargaining and compromise. The role of industrial relations is, then, to reach mutually agreed solutions to clashes of interest. Fox made a sharp distinction between the two perspectives. Doing so is always a good way of helping people to become conscious of the assumptions that they make: the typical managerial assumption is of a unity of interests. However, the approach of management to employee relations is more varied today than this distinction would suggest.

Five different types of approach to managing industrial relations are suggested by Purcell and Sisson.[18] They call these ideal rather than actual types. These are useful for highlighting different managerial approaches and for helping managers to recognize what approach is used in their own organization. The first is called 'traditionalist', in which management forcefully opposes trade unions and often overtly exploits the employees. The image is of the nineteenth-century capitalist entrepreneur, although the attitude still exists in places. The second is the 'sophisticated paternalist', exemplified by IBM, Hewlett-Packard, Kodak and Marks & Spencer. Purcell and Sisson comment:

> The sophisticated paternalists do not take it for granted that their employees accept the company's objectives or automatically legitimize management decision-making; they spend considerable time and resources in ensuring that their employees have the right approach. Recruitment, selection, training, counseling, high pay and fringe benefits – these and other personal policies are used to ensure that individual aspirations are mostly satisfied, that collective action is seen as unnecessary and inappropriate.[19]

The third type covers the 'sophisticated moderns', who recognize that union participation in some aspects of joint decision-making has advantages for management: for instance, in promoting consent and the handling of change. The authors divide the 'sophisticated moderns' into two groups, which they call 'constitutionalists' and 'consultors'. The former are much more common in the USA than in the UK and are based on the idea that, outside collective agreements, management is free to take its own decisions. The latter include companies like ICI and most of the large oil companies. These do not want to codify everything in collective agreement. Their emphasis is on solving problems rather than on settling disputes. Procedures for consultation are 'usually extremely detailed and wide-ranging in communications and interpersonal skills'.[20]

Both the sophisticated paternalists and the sophisticated moderns have a fairly uniform approach throughout the organization, and one that has continued for many years. Individual managers are expected to conform to the company's general approach. This contrasts with the last group, the 'standard moderns', which are pragmatic or opportunistic. The examples given are the General Electric Company in the UK, Guest, Keen and Nettlefolds, and Tube Investments. Trade unions are recognized, but unlike the other two groups there does not seem to be a common set of values. Hence managers differ in their approach to industrial relations.

Purcell and Sisson explain the differences in approach as

primarily due to the attitudes of key personalities at an early stage in the company's development. In the pragmatic 'standard modern' companies the authors could not identify such personalities in the early stages.

How is management likely to exercise authority in the future? There seems little to suggest that many companies will practise effective participative management, which requires both a belief that it is right to do so (which is becoming more common) as well as personalities that can cope with the problems inherent in any genuine attempt to encourage employees to share in some aspects of decision-making. Participative management will not work well just because it is law or because management thinks it will pay. Managers who do not genuinely believe that people have a right to share in decisions affecting them are likely to be irritated by the difficulties that arise in discussions.

In exercising authority managers take many things for granted. A British manager, for instance, used to a society with a long industrial history, will take for granted a workforce that is adapted to industry: that is, one which expects to work regularly and to take orders about the methods and pace of work. Technology has increasingly reduced the opportunities for individuals to behave differently from each other at work, as specialized production requires that people work in a prescribed manner and therefore be subject to external, rather than internal, discipline. British managers who go to an underdeveloped country find that employees are used to an agricultural society. It is one that gives labourers far more control over the way in which, and the pace at which, they work. Hence the assumptions that managers use to guide them in Britain will no longer be valid. This may cause less difficulty in underdeveloped countries than in other industrial countries, such as France or Italy, where the differences are smaller but may be more difficult to spot. Countries like Nigeria or Peru are so obviously different from Britain that managers may expect differences in employees' attitudes and be prepared to rethink some aspects of their relations with employees. Because the relation between management and worker varies in different countries, most companies operating in other industrial countries try, if they can, to recruit local management to deal with labour.

Labour's attitude to management

The way in which management exercises its authority, and the social structure within which it does so, will largely determine labour's view of management. For instance, the attitude of the Japanese workers to their manager will be quite different from that of the British or American.

The extent of national differences in workers' attitudes to management can be illustrated by a study by Duncan Gallie of workers' attitudes in four oil refineries belonging to the same company in France and Britain. This study found that the former took a much more critical view of management than did the latter.[21] The British were found to be broadly content with their incomes and standard of living, while the French were dissatisfied. They resented their situation as manual workers in French society. They were also 'deeply convinced that the principles determining salary allocation within the industry were unfair; the British, on the other hand were overwhelmingly satisfied with them'.[22] The French workers were much more militant about shift-working and manning. The criticisms that the French and British workers made of management also differed. The main French criticism was of the high degree of social distance that existed between management and workers: 'Management was seen as aloof and cold, fundamentally uninterested in the workers as human beings.' The British criticisms were primarily technical ones of management's efficiency, though these were not accompanied by a demand for more control by the workers. The British workers saw management as working in the interests of everyone, while the French workers saw management as exploitive, being primarily concerned with the shareholders' interests. This was illustrated by their attitudes to power and control, as Gallie says:

> The French felt that the existing structure of power was illegitimate, and a clear majority would have been prepared to see an extension of worker control over management's powers of decision into the very heart of the traditional areas of managerial prerogative, including the most fundamental strategic decisions about financial budgeting and new investment. In contrast, the British workers showed a high level of contentment with the existing procedures of decision making.

Gallie suggests that the difference in attitudes may be partly explained by the fact that the French managers remained sovereign at the refinery, while in the British refineries the shop-floor representatives had control, in the sense of a power of veto, over many aspects of work organization. This study was published in 1978 but no later study is known which could tell us whether similar differences continue to exist.

Labour's attitudes to management differ in different countries. There are also industrial differences that at least partially cut across national boundaries, as strike figures show. Many people, including managers in strike-free companies, say that managers get the labour relations they deserve. This is only a half truth, for it is much harder to have good industrial relations in some industries than in others. A good management may be handicapped by a legacy of bad relations in the company, which may take years to live down, or by being in an industry with a long record of bad relations.

There are many ways by which workers can express their dissatisfaction with their management including: absenteeism, industrial disputes including strikes, stealing and sabotage. Whether they feel dissatisfied and how they choose to express this will depend upon many factors. There are management attitudes and personnel policies. There is the nature of the work – is it in itself likely to be satisfying? There is the employment situation – is leaving easy? There is the industrial relations history and the bargaining power of those who are dissatisfied.

Two major and related changes have affected whether dissatisfaction shows itself in industrial conflict. One is the change in the nature of jobs: far fewer in manufacturing and far more in the service industries; more part-time jobs held by women and fewer jobs for men with no qualifications. The other is the decline in trade unionism, which provided the organization for industrial conflict: in the UK at the end of 1994 there were 8.3 million trade union members compared with the 13.3 million in the peak year, 1979.[23] These two changes are reflected in the decline of collective bargaining and the increase in individual employment contracts. The expression of dissatisfaction is, therefore, more an individual reaction and less a collective one. The optimists would argue that there is less to be dissatisfied about as traditional assembly line jobs are changed to membership of self-directed work teams, and management's stress empowerment. Pessimists can point to the long hours worked by many technical, professional and managerial staff and to the demanding work schedules in manufacturing.

Summary

Why managers think and act as they do depends partly on the type of people they are, but more on their environment. This is made up of the social and economic history of the country in which they are working, including the stage of industrialization; the position of business in society; the prevailing moral standards; the relation of the social classes; the strength of the trade union movement; and the number and type of government regulations. Both the methods of conducting business and the attitudes to employees will mainly depend on what is customary at that time and place.

   The educational and social background of managers varies in different countries. This is one reason why the approach of the French or German manager tends to be different from that of the British, and all three of them different from the Japanese. In some countries the family still plays a dominant role, although its influence is now small in the USA and the UK. Even so, in both countries managers' social background still has an influence on their chances of becoming a manager. The professional background of a manager can also influence his or her view of management. In Germany, where engineers play a big role in management, the approach to business is likely to differ from Britain, where accountants are more favoured for top management. The Japanese and the German are more task-oriented and more egalitarian in their relations with workers than the British.

   How management exercises authority differs over time, as well as between countries. One factor influencing it is the width of the social gap that exists between management and workers. In some countries managers still receive a feudal deference from their workers. With increasing industrialization management's authority declines, partly because a rising standard of living reduces the social distance between management and workers, partly because trade unions and government regulations restrict management's freedom of action. Five different approaches to industrial relations today were described. Most stem from the values held by a key figure in company history.

Labour's attitude to management is a response to how management treats the workers. It is also a reflection of the social structure. There are marked differences between industries as well as between countries, and in the same country at different periods in its history. Today many employees would not see themselves as 'labour' but as middle class staff. They are likely to have an individual contract with their employer and are less likely than in the past to belong to a trade union. When they are dissatisfied with their employer they are more likely to quit than to strike, unless they belong to a group with sufficient solidarity to take collective action.

9 Management in large organizations

What difference does size make to the problems of managing people and getting organizations to work effectively? This is the question that we shall address in this chapter. It is an important one because large organizations form a substantial part of the economy. Some management problems become more difficult in large organizations, others become easier, while yet others are a mixture of the two. We shall briefly review the advantages, then concentrate on the disadvantages in the belief that a clearer awareness of what they are, and of what may be done to lessen them, is needed.

The advantages of large organizations

The main financial and technical advantages of large companies – the reasons for many mergers and take-overs – are the: economics of large-scale production; easier access to finance; spread of risks, including better opportunities for diversification; and ability to undertake very expensive technical tasks. The last can be a key reason for mergers in industries that have a heavy expenditure on research and development. There are also important marketing reasons for acquiring companies overseas in an increasingly global marketplace. An advantage of being a very large company is that it is more powerful and, therefore, less likely to be taken over. Even so, size does not guarantee protection, as many large companies have found.

One of the most important advantages of a large firm, according to Edwards and Townsend, writing over thirty years ago, is that its size enables exceptional managerial abilities to be used to the full.[1] There is, however, the corresponding disadvantage that managers with exceptional abilities are scarce, and a large organization that does not have outstanding managers may run into difficulties. Its managers might be completely satisfactory in a smaller company but not be able to cope successfully with the scale of problems in a large organization. It is one's estimate of the supply of exceptional managerial ability that will determine whether one agrees with Edwards and Townsend's arguments. Certainly, the anxiety shown by some of the most successful large companies about how to get good top managers suggests that the supply is too small to meet the demand. Occasionally outstanding managers are found in medium-sized companies, where their abilities may be restricted by lack of capital. Then a merger with a larger company can give them greater scope.

Today the importance still attached to exceptional managerial talent is shown by the effects that the appointment of a well-regarded chief executive can have on the share price. This is particularly true of ailing companies. The greater complexity of business today may make exceptional managerial talent even more important than in the past. 'May' because large companies are often divided into smaller subsidiaries, which are allowed a lot of independence provided they are profitable. The growth of service industries and the decline in large-scale manufacturing has made this way of organizing large companies much easier.

The large firm usually has an advantage in recruiting staff, especially for management posts. Many people prefer to be associated with a large, well-known company for its reputation (outside people will have heard of the company where they work), for its better facilities, greater security (less true than it used to be) and better opportunities for promotion to interesting and well-paid jobs. The large company is also able to spend more time and money on trying to attract the people it wants. It will have an advantage in promotion, too, because it will have a bigger pool on which to draw, particularly for management posts. Although the big company has an advantage in recruitment, there are people at all levels who will prefer to work for a small or medium-sized one.

The disadvantages of large organizations

The greatest problem of large-scale organization is how to prevent feelings of indifference or frustration. Junior and

middle management may feel frustrated because they are a
long way from effective authority, though reduction in the
number of management hierarchies, 'delayering', has made
this less of a problem than in the past. Workers, both manual
and clerical, may feel little or no identification with the
company where they work. All may miss the feeling of
personal loyalty and commitment that can come from working
for 'the boss'. Even the chief executive may feel frustrated
because of the number of people who may need to be
consulted before an important decision is taken.

It is lower down the management hierarchy that feelings
of frustration are most likely. These may be caused by long
delays in getting a decision, by poor communication with
related departments, and by uncertainties about the scope
of the person's authority. Each additional level in the management hierarchy is a potential obstacle to communication.
Each reduces the responsibility of those below, so that those
at the bottom of the management ladder, or even part of the
way up, may feel frustrated by the small opportunity for exercising responsibility. How serious this feeling is likely to be
will depend on the number of management levels, the extent
of centralization, and on the consistency and clarity of the
policies for what decisions can be taken at different levels.

Managers' jobs in large organizations are more specialized
than their counterpart in a small, or medium-sized, under-
taking. Hence it is harder for them to get experience
of different functions, or to have much conception of the
business as a whole. So long as they remain in middle management, this may not matter, but those who are promoted
to top management will need a wider experience and knowledge, which companies that take management development
seriously will seek to provide. Another, related, difficulty of
large organizations is that some of those who might make
good top managers are not prepared for the time it can still
take to get to senior positions in large organizations, even
though fewer tiers and earlier retirements have made it easier
to reach the top younger. Hence some keen young people
will opt for smaller companies, or for consulting firms, where
they can make a mark more quickly and get a wide experience of management, which will be useful later if they want
to move.

A feeling among junior and lower-middle managers that they are far removed from effective authority is one of the dangers of large organizations. This feeling can be more pronounced on the shop floor, which may be faced with a local management that does not have the authority to give a decision on a question raised by the union or by workers' representatives.

A frequently mentioned problem of large organizations is the difficulties of creating or maintaining good management–worker relations. The interest in incentives, and in ways of encouraging greater management–worker cooperation, all stem from the divorce between the two, which can develop as a firm grows larger. In the smallest firm, such as a small builder and decorator, the workers may identify themselves with the business. As it grows from 5 employees to 50, from 50 to 100 and from 100 to 500, there will be changes in the relation between the boss and employees, even if the boss remains the same. Above about 600 employees no manager can really know all the employees; hence that form of personal knowledge comes to an end. Employees' feelings of personal responsibility for the success of the company diminish as the company grows: whether they are late or absent becomes a purely personal question that may be affected by penalties for bad timekeeping rather than by a concern for any disruption they may cause.

Lack of commitment to the organization can show itself in various ways in: absenteeism, the accident rate, industrial disputes and a high turnover. The size of the organization may, depending upon the way in which it is organized and how it has grown, have an important effect on the commitment to it of the junior and middle managers. The size of the establishment where they work, that is, the individual producing unit, whether factory, colliery, power station, retail store or hospital, is more important in its effects on workers' commitment than the size of the organization as a whole.

A study of industrial disputes in Britain between mid-1979 and mid-1980 – called 'the winter of discontent' – concluded that 'there is a strong relationship between the occurrence of every type of industrial action and the number of manual workers at the establishment'.[2] This is strikingly shown in Table 9.1. The authors suggest that there is a 'threshold effect', as some forms of industrial action are only possible when a certain number of workers are in a single establishment. There have been fewer strikes since then, but this example of the greater problems of management–worker relationships in large establishments is still a reminder that managers in large establishments have to work harder to enlist commitment.

So far we have not mentioned what are traditionally supposed to be the disadvantages of large organization: inflexibility, red-tape, and empire-building. The amount of formal information, whether on paper or disks, must go up as an organization grows as a substitute for personal knowledge and word of mouth. Both the amount of paper and the rate of empire-building may be increased if managers feel insecure; they may record everything to protect themselves, or build empires to bolster their prestige. Yet the dangers of red-tape and empire-building in large organizations can be held in check and the more determined drive in business and the public service in the 1980s and 1990s to cut costs has led to drastic slimming of many large organizations. E-mail has also helped reduce the paper and contributed to greater informality.

More difficult problems to be overcome are inflexibility and delay. The process of working out the general aims of the organization, getting agreement for changes, keeping each part of the organization informed, and checking it if it departs

Table 9.1 Percentage of industrial action by manual workers between mid-1979 and mid-1980 by the number of manual workers in the establishment

	Any type of industrial action (%)	Strike/lockout (%)
Total	**18**	**12**
No. of manual workers:		
1–9	2	2
10–24	8	5
25–49	13	8
50–99	27	18
100–199	33	21
200–499	50	40
500–999	74	53
1000+	77	67

from the common aims and plan, is a laborious one. There may be so many people to be consulted before an important decision is made that it can take much longer in a large company than in a medium-sized one. As long ago as 1925 Alfred E. Sloan, chairman of General Motors, bemoaned that:

> In practically all our activities we seem to suffer from the inertia resulting from our great size. It seems to be hard for us to get action when it comes to a matter of putting our ideas across. There are so many people involved and it requires such a tremendous effort to put something new into effect, that a new idea is likely to be considered insignificant in comparison with the effort that it takes to put it across.
> ... Sometimes I am almost forced to the conclusion that General Motors is so large that it is impossible for us to really be leaders.[3]

Nor are the problems of inertia likely to be so different in today's large organizations. All of them have to cope with the fact that the amount of energy required to oppose is much less than that required to initiate and carry through a change. How much inertia and resistance there will be depends partly upon the background and calibre of the people recruited, partly on the culture of the organization and partly on how used its managers are to change. It is the last point, plus greater competition and job insecurity, that has made it easier for change to be accepted. Now managers, and other staff too, have become conditioned to accept change as an aspect of modern organizational life, but large organizations still have more problems in getting change really accepted.

Different ways of being big

So far we have talked about the problems of large-scale organizations as if they were common to all large companies. So indeed they are, but their intensity will vary according to how the firm has grown, how it is organized, and what stage it has reached in its history. Organizations can become big in different ways: they can grow gradually, like Shell Petroleum, or with great rapidity, like the latest, and often short-lived, stock market star. Large organizations can be created by the amalgamation of a small number of fair-sized companies, which was the origin of ICI, or, in the days of nationalization, they became big overnight as when 800 companies were changed into the National Coal Board. The difficulties experienced in the early days of the large nationalized industries in the UK were particularly acute because of the huge and sudden increase in the size of the organization. Unhappily, the decades since then provide similar, if less acute, examples of the problems of large organizations, especially those formed by mergers and take-overs.

Companies may continue to grow by mergers and take-overs as well as by expansion of existing resources. In the USA expenditure on acquisitions in recent years has been about half that on new plant and equipment.[4] In the UK, expenditure on acquisitions has varied widely. Take-overs are popular with the Anglo-Saxon economies, rare in Japan and much less common in France, Italy and Germany. There seems little evidence to support the enthusiasm for take-overs, since performance has been disappointing and many have later been sold. The explanation seems to be too optimistic a view of the benefits of the take-over and a failure to anticipate the subsequent problems of controlling the new subsidiaries.[5]

Rapid growth intensifies management problems of coordination and human relations because tradition can play little or no part. Much of the work of an organization is carried out through informal contact. But in an organization created by amalgamation there will be no common network and its growth will inevitably take time. A lengthy mutual process of getting to know one another, both in terms of recognition and of assessment, will have to go on. In some ways a company that expands very rapidly has fewer problems than one that is created by amalgamations, or grows through mergers, because it will have a core of people who know each other on which to build. In other ways it can be more difficult, because the changes that have to be made may be less obvious than they are in an amalgamation.

Any take-over creates problems of how to fit the new company into the existing structure. The parent, unless it is only a financial holding company, will seek, to a greater or lesser extent, to mould the new acquisition to the parental pattern. The technical, financial and administrative changes may amount to almost complete integration or only to control of selected aspects of the business. In theory these changes need not take long but, if the management of the parent organization is anxious not to kill the growing tree in the process, not to destroy management initiative and enthusiasm, they will have to be made slowly. Unless it is a relatively small acquisition, the parent company may also gradually change during the process of adjustment. Hence the necessity, underlined by a number of organizations with experience of take-overs, for allowing sufficient time for digestion before embarking on a large new one

A major factor restricting the growth of companies in recent years has been cost cutting and restructuring to cut the number of staff and the number of tiers in the management hierarchy. Increasingly, another factor is the growth of outsourcing. A quite different factor is the recent splitting of large companies, which contain very different businesses, into separate, more homogeneous ones. ICI was a leader in this when it split into ICI and Zeneca. More recently, in 1996, Thorn EMI also split into two and there are a number of other examples.

Whatever the difficulties for management created by large-scale organization, they did not prevent many large firms from growing still larger. The financial and technical advantages of size were usually sufficient to outweigh the disadvantages. The share of the 100 largest firms in UK manufacturing net output during the period 1909–70 rose from 15 per cent to 45 per cent.[6] In the recession of the late seventies and early eighties many large organizations were cut back. Others continued to expand, so that the numbers of firms employing over 10,000 remained more or less constant. The changes described above mean that the number of employees is no longer a good guide to the size of the firm. A firm can now be very large by financial measures but have well below 10,000 employees. So some of the disadvantages of large organizations described earlier are less widespread than before. However, it is still important to examine what can be done to reduce these disadvantages, and especially their disadvantages for the employee, whether manager or worker.

What can be done?

The list of disadvantages of large-scale organizations is a long one: a many-tiered management structure, with its dangers of poor communication and a feeling of remoteness from effective authority; junior and middle managers who feel that they do not have enough responsibility; specialists who feel frustrated because their advice is not taken; workers who feel their contribution does not matter and who become indifferent to the success of the company; inflexibility, form-filling, and empire-building. Yet even then the list is not exhaustive. These are dangers inherent in large-scale organizations, but they can all be mitigated if not avoided. They are problems that may have to be lived with, but that can be kept in check by awareness and watchfulness. Some problems can even be averted: there are large companies with excellent labour relations.

Much can be done, by the philosophy and policies of management and by changes in the organization structure, to reduce the human disadvantages of bigness. In the list of disadvantages in the previous paragraph the word 'feel' recurs. People in large organizations can more easily feel unimportant, insecure and, if they are managers, uncertain of their authority or prospects. But it is not inevitable that they should feel like that in a large organization. A management that really believes that people are individuals, and that individuals matter, can constantly seek to give effect to this belief. It may, for instance, experiment with increasing the content of jobs if it thinks that people find their jobs too narrow. It can promote those who share its belief in the importance of individuals.

One of the ways in which the anonymity of top management – with all its possible implications of a lack of feeling – may be lessened, even in the largest organization, is by the actions of the chief executive. If he or she really cares about individuals, and is able to make this public knowledge, it can influence the attitudes of employees at all levels. This was strikingly shown in one company where the managing director not merely cared deeply about the welfare of his employees, but wrote and broadcast about his philosophy of management so that many of his employees had heard of it. He also made a point of visiting any newly acquired company and meeting many of its employees. The result was that a number of the managers in these companies, when interviewed about their reactions to the merger, said that they felt they could go to the managing director if they had a complaint and get a fair deal. Another managing director regarded appearances on television as one way of being known to employees.

Much can also be done by the form of the organization to prevent people from feeling frustrated. Companies with small working groups and small establishments will tend to have fewer problems with staff morale and cooperation than those with large establishments and large working groups. The nature of its business will determine what choice a company has in this aspect of its organization, but at least managers should be aware of the importance of any element of choice there may be.

Good human relations requires more conscious thought and effort in a large organization than in a small one, where the right attitude can take a manager much further. In a large organization managers need to understand the possible sources of frustration. They may not see the symptoms of frustration until they show in lost-time rates, high labour turnover, strikes and management ulcers. A manager who remembers, for instance, that a long delay in getting a decision, uncertainty about the scope of one's authority or the views of one's superior can be frustrating will take more trouble to avoid these than an equally well-intentioned manager who does not.

Many problems are intensified in a highly centralized organization which encourages red-tape and resistance to change and which gives the more junior managers little opportunity to exercise responsibility. Therefore, an important organizational aim is to centralize as little as possible and to keep the number of tiers in the management hierarchy to the minimum. But the 'as possible' is important. What is possible will vary at different periods in a company's history. More centralization may be necessary in the early days of a merger than later.

How much decentralization is possible also varies in different industries; the opportunities for it are obviously less in oil refining or in steel making than in industries where production can economically be broken down into separate units. Some companies are inescapably committed to large establishments, which are probably more important factors in morale than the size of the company. Others may have some choice both in the size of their establishments and in whether they divide their company – as so many success-ful large companies are divided – into semi-autonomous subsidiaries or divisions. If it is possible to judge the profit-ability of a subsidiary, it is easier to go further in decen-tralization, as it can then be treated in many ways as a separate economic unit.

The minimum of centralization that is customary in a large organization is financial control over capital expenditure above a stated figure, approval of financial budgets, control over top level appointments and remuneration, and, in a unionized company, probably the conduct of national trade union negotiations. There may also be a staff of specialists at headquarters, although many companies now limit their head office to the staff necessary to operate these central controls. According to Edwards and Townsend:

> Provided one decides rightly which types of decisions to allow to come to the centre there is no reason why the problem of coordination should make a large firm less efficient than two or more smaller, independent firms. This does not mean that no large firms will suffer from unwieldiness, woolliness and slowness; but if they do so it will be because of deficiencies in particular managements, not because of the inevitable defi-ciencies of large organizations. Small firms may equally suffer from deficiencies in management and very frequently do.

There is no stage at which an organization must become less efficient than it would be if it were smaller; but beyond the point where economies of large outputs and cost-reducing advantages of large organizations are exhausted it will not be more efficient.[7]

It is arguable whether good organization – meaning, espe-cially here, the right balance between centralization and decentralization – can overcome all the disadvantages of co-ordination in large organizations, as Edwards and Townsend claim. The problem of the number of people to be consulted must still remain, as must that of keeping all parts of the organization informed when necessary. That large firms can be efficient and small firms inefficient is clear, but to manage a large company as efficiently as a small one requires a higher calibre of management. The same is true for other kinds of organizations, such as hospitals or schools.

Summary

The number and size of large companies shows that economically their advantages outweigh their disadvantages, though the sceptic may say that the ability of the large fish to swallow the small is no reflection on the efficient functioning of the latter. Despite its economic advantages, a large organization has inherent difficulties, which its managers must combat. To do so successfully requires better managers than in a smaller company. The large company is fortunate in being in a stronger position for recruiting such men and women.

One of the greatest problems of large-scale organization is how to prevent feelings of indifference or frustration. Staff may feel that their contribution does not matter and that nobody cares about them. They will find it hard to identify with the success of the organization. Managers may be frustrated because of delays in getting a decision, or because of poor communication. They may feel that they do not have enough responsibility; in part because of the number of tiers in the management structure, and in part because of problems of communication, even with the developments in information technology. Promotion may be slow, and it is harder for managers in large organizations than in smaller ones to get experience for top management.

The traditional temptations of large-scale organization are inflexibility, red-tape and empire-building. These dangers can be kept in check, although never abolished. But the inertia level of large organizations may always be higher than that of the efficient small company.

Although there are common problems of bigness, they will be more intense in some companies than others. It depends how the company has become big. If it has grown rapidly, whether by amalgamation or natural expansion, its problems will be greater than those of a company that has grown gradually, building on, and developing its tradition as it grows.

It is obvious that some large organizations keep many of these problems under control. Their management philosophy and policies help to prevent people feeling unimportant, insecure and frustrated. In a few the chief executive's obvious personal concern for the staff can do much to reassure them that 'the boss' does care. The type of organization can also help to prevent a feeling of remoteness; as far as possible, there should be small groups, small establishments and a decentralized organization. It is the size of the individual establishments that is most important in its effects on morale As Dr E. Schumacher said 'the fundamental task is to achieve smallness within the organization'.[8]

10 The manager and change

This chapter is in two parts. The first describes the major changes affecting management and what can be done to plan for them. The second discusses what has been learnt about how to implement change successfully.

Many of the realities of management change little or are modified gradually, but some are revolutionized. This is true of the extent to which companies, even very large companies, are vulnerable to external changes. Sudden changes in the supply of essential raw materials such as oil can provide a dramatic example, but there are many other unexpected changes as managers in more and more companies have to seek for their business overseas and to face competition from the old and the newly industrialized countries. Changes in technology and in domestic government policies have also had a radical impact on managers in many companies and in public service organizations.

One of the most difficult problems for managers is rapid change. How British managers react to change will have an important influence on Britain's economic future. This is true for managers in the public service as well as for those in industry and commerce. The tempo of change has speeded up; hence the demands made on managers to plan for, and adjust to, change are greater. All change requires both abilities. Some changes can be planned for in great detail, such as the switch to a new model. Others may be unforeseeable, but if the organization is kept sufficiently flexible, it will be able to cope with the unexpected. The number of completely unexpected changes can be kept to a minimum by foresight. Changes also mean adjustment. Without it the planning will be unsuccessful. Adjustment is usually more difficult for managers than planning, because it has an emotional aspect to it, for them individually, for their peers, and for their staff. They have to be able to acclimatize both themselves and their staff to the change.

The sources of major change affecting management are:

1 Political changes which can have a major effect on the public service, but may also change the context in which industry and commerce operate.
2 Greater competition both at home and abroad.
3 The business cycle, particularly severe declines in the stock market.
4 Sudden changes affecting particular industries.
5 Innovations that lead to new products and new methods of working as well as making some current products obsolete.
6 Changes in consumer expenditure as a result of innovations, of changes in consumer wants and of new methods of selling.
7 Changes in the background, training and occupation of those employed.
8 Industrial action.
9 New social changes, such as the growth of the green movement and the pressure for equal opportunities for women and ethnic minorities.
10 The growth of information technology.

Let us look at each of these in turn to see how they affect management and what can be done to prevent, or more usually to limit, their effects

Changes affecting management

Political changes

The government can affect the work of managers in a number of ways, but most commonly by changing taxation affecting companies and by introducing employment legislation. It can also make changes that have a more direct impact on a large number of managers' jobs. It can change the structure and ownership of an organization by nationalization and privatization. It can influence the amount of competition by regulating take-overs and by appointing regulators for privatized industries. It can reorganize public service organizations. It can change the rules within which different types of businesses have operated for many years, as it has those affecting financial institutions. In Britain in the first half of the eighties the effects of political changes on management were greater than they had been since the nationalization measures of the first post-war Labour government. A radical Conservative government sought to make managers in the public service more aware that they *were* managers, and hence more accountable. It sought to make changes that would improve the efficiency of public services and of private industry. In New Zealand, at a similar time, radical changes were introduced affecting managers, particularly in the public sector, which in some ways went further than those introduced in Britain. In the Greater London Council, before it was abolished, a radical Labour administration also changed many officers' work by its determination to see its policies implemented, including its support for the employment opportunities of minority groups and of women.

Many companies are now affected by political changes overseas. In the past it was mainly industries like oil where management had to be so concerned about the effects of political changes overseas. Now all companies in the EC have to be alert to decisions made in Brussels, but with increasingly international markets what happens in many other countries matters too.

The political changes affecting managers in the public sector have been so great in the 1980s and 1990s, particularly privatization and radical changes to the remaining public sector, that they merit being listed first among the changes affecting managers. Managers in many companies are more affected by changes in technology, markets and in the economy.

Some political changes can be anticipated by managers and plans made accordingly. A few may be prevented or modified by lobbying, but, for most, planning is limited to dealing with the consequences.

Greater competition

Competition has become much more international as the Far Eastern economies have developed rapidly and as companies operate more worldwide. Competition from Japan and later

Korea and other Far Eastern countries was a major reason for the contraction that managers in many manufacturing companies had to carry through. More managers became experienced in managing rundown. The pressure of competition provided the stimulus to managers in many different industries to try to improve the efficiency of their operations. It was also the reason for a greater interest in strategic planning, as more managers realized the need to assess the strengths and weaknesses, threats and opportunities facing their companies. The problems of the European economies, in the face of Asian and American competition, also affected the public services, as governments looked for ways of economizing. Managers in all kinds of organizations needed to become better at managing their resources and were more likely than in the past to be penalized if they did not.

The business cycle

Boom and bust or at least periods of high demand alternating with slack demand are a well-known feature of the business environment. Newspapers carry frequent accounts of changes in consumer demand, prospects for the housing market and whether the stock markets are too high and likely to tumble. Despite all the economic research there are no sure predictions for the onset of a recession.

The more flexible employment policies followed by many companies today make it easier to adjust the number of employees to sudden changes in demand. Some companies may also seek to mitigate the severity of the adjustments by diversification to products that operate on a different cycle as some experience a recession later than others.

Sudden changes affecting particular industries

Disaster can strike an industry unexpectedly. Health scares can have a sudden and major effect on the prosperity of an industry as BSE (mad cow disease) had on beef farmers and all companies involved in the beef industry. Tobacco and the pharmaceutical industry are more used to the effects of health scares on their industry via compensation claims or new legislation. The insurance industry must expect unusually high claims from time to time.

Innovations

Innovations may also destroy an industry, but usually this takes time so there is more possibility of adapting than for the sudden disasters described above. The tempo of innovation is much greater than before; hence in some industries a company must spend heavily on research and development if it is to survive. To avoid stagnation or decline it must ever be on the look-out for new possibilities for growth as the leading areas of growth change within a few years. This is true in manufacturing and in services. Hence one of the important problems for management is to make certain that it adapts its products fast enough to meet changes in demand.

Diversification into other industries, and into other parts of the same industry, is one answer to the need to protect the company from a decline in its products. There is a danger, however, that a company may diversify without sufficient study of what products and markets are likely to grow, and of which ones are suitable for the company – suitable in terms of its capital, location, access to raw materials, and managerial know-how. In diversification by merger the latter will be enlarged by the experience of the managers in the other company. This may provide a solution to the problem of inadequate managerial know-how in the new industry, provided the acquiring company can retain the key people.

Innovation in some industries, such as pharmaceuticals, is a lengthy business, so the company will have to plan well ahead. In selecting a research project it will have to judge the following: the likelihood of success; the time it will take; and its costs and its value, judged by the likely market gain and by the need for a new or improved product. The latter will mainly depend on the competitive position and the rate of obsolescence of existing products. Completing the research project and deciding to manufacture a new product are only the first stages in launching a new product. Management may be stronger at one stage of the process of innovation than at another. They may, for instance, be better at analysing a problem and reaching a decision than they are at getting sufficient agreement to make the implementation successful. Or they may get into difficulties at the implementation stage because top management considers speed synonymous with efficiency and, therefore, tends to skimp the preliminary stages. The launching of a new product may also come to grief because of the way in which it is marketed. Selling a new product may mean entering a new market and competing against those familiar with it. Curiously, some companies plan the design and manufacture of a new product with great care, but treat the marketing of it as if it was a routine matter, although the market they are entering may need quite different methods from their customary ones. They may also attach too much importance to the goodwill their name has earned elsewhere, but which may have little value in a new market where others are already established. There is also the opposite danger of concentrating too much on the marketing and too little on the timing and quality of production.

The chances of future success would be greater if companies more often analysed the causes of their failure. It is useful to find out at what stage the project ran into difficulties. This may show up a recurrent weakness at a particular stage. Unfortunately management is often chary of analysing the causes of failure, because it will not face up to the fact of failure, because it is afraid of upsetting people or because it does not see such analysis to be important.

Changes in consumer expenditure

The pattern of consumer expenditure changes rapidly. The age distribution of the population, the age of marriage, the average number of children and how soon after marriage they are born, the proportion of women working, the level of education, the amount of leisure, and the availability of goods, all have changed in recent years and all influence what consumers buy and when. A major factor determining how money is spent is the standard of living and how it is distributed between occupations and between age groups. Another is changes in fashions, such as the growth of informality and its effects on what people wear – look down a street in many cities in the world and see what the popularity of jeans must have done to makers of skirts and dresses and tailored trousers!

The company that correctly foresees future consumer wants can get into a growing market at the beginning. It might take as a general guide that today's affluent consumer is tomorrow's average consumer, although it should check on how many other manufacturers are acting on the same principle. An alternative approach is niche marketing, which requires identifying specialist interests and can be a good starting point for a new business.

Changes in the composition of the working force

At the beginning of the twentieth century the majority of American people lived in rural settlements and made a living from farming. By 1940 this group had been overtaken by industrial, especially semi-skilled, workers. The picture had changed again by 1960 when the largest single group was 'professional, managerial, and technical people'.[1] By the 1980s this group comprised the majority of working Americans. This means that the education, occupation and outlook of the people that managers are working with, whether as staff or colleagues, has changed. Drucker highlighted how management is affected, when much of its time is spent managing knowledge workers. He says:

> The position of these people, however, we do not yet fully understand. Nor do we know how to manage them, that is, how to make their knowledge, their efforts, their contribution effective in the performance of the whole. This is a problem which few, if any, of the founding fathers of management could have foreseen, it is a problem that only arose because they were so successful. But as problems of success usually are, this is more difficult, at least a much more subtle, problem than any they tackled.[2]

Industrial action

The changes in the composition of the workforce and the resulting decline in the number of trade unionists has contributed to a reduction in the number of industrial disputes. So, in Britain, did the legislation passed by the Thatcher government which introduced new constraints on the actions of trade unions. In consequence of these changes

British managers have had to face less uncertainty from industrial action than from the other sources of change. Even so, the situation can change. It is always an area of potential threat to the smooth running of organizations, particularly in the public sector as the 1996 strikes in the London Underground and the Post Office showed. Even if managers are lucky enough or able enough to avoid industrial action in their own organizations, they may still need to plan for the effects of industrial action taken elsewhere. An understanding of the causes of these actions, and the skill to prevent them where possible and to mitigate their effects where not, are still requirements for the effective manager today.

New social changes

Managers operate in a world where social conditions and social expectations are always changing. There are the long-run changes resulting from a better education and a higher standard of living that affect people's expectations both as employees – the word 'subordinate' now has an alien ring for many people – and as consumers. Two more recent changes that are affecting management are: one, the demands for equality of opportunity for women, for ethnic minorities and for the disabled, and two, the ideas behind the green movement which are requiring companies to be more careful of the effects of their activities on the natural environment. Managers have to take these social changes seriously or be increasingly required to do so.

The growth of information technology

Today managers need to understand how to use information technology (IT) and the contribution that it can make to the solution of some of their problems. 'Information technology' is a general term for computers and other methods of handling information electronically. Computers can help managers' own work in different ways: by providing regular reports for monitoring what is happening, by greatly increasing managers' ability to ask for special information, to tap new sources of information, and by making possible much more complicated analyses of what is happening or what might happen. Many questions can be answered now that could not have been answered before. Many strategic possibilities can be explored now that would have been too difficult before. But for much of this to be useful managers must know what questions to ask, be interested in asking them and know what to do with the results.

The rapid developments in IT mean that earlier predictions about the impact of computers on management are irrelevant. So, probably, are any attempts to make predictions now. We know that IT can facilitate greater decentralization: top management can now more quickly monitor what it wants to control and leave staff to run their profit centres. We know also that IT investments, like other large investments, can be costly failures because the potential value is overestimated and the costs and difficulties are underestimated. There are plenty of horror stories to support that gloomy statement. We know that information, more than ever before, has become a resource that has to be managed and is often poorly managed. Many managers prefer to get their information from people. They do not know how to make the best use of the computer. This is more true for top managers than for middle managers. Some, but by no means all, middle managers do make substantial use of computers to provide them with the information that they want. Most top managers are not significant users. The jury is still out on whether they will become significant users. Some argue that they will as soon as those who are familiar with computers and their potential reach top management posts. Others argue that computers can contribute little to top management.[3]

Managing change

Resistance to change

There are two main problems in the successful implementation of change: that the changes that are necessary are not recognized or that they are resisted. Good planning will help to prevent the first, but, if the change is to be successful, people at all levels in the organization must make the necessary adjustments, and make them in time to avoid costly delays. A knowledge of the most common causes of resistance to change can be helpful for appreciating what opposition is likely to be met and why.

The place of one occupation in relation to others, in terms of remuneration, perks and prestige, may become established over the years. Rapid change frequently means a shift in the relative importance of occupations, the creation of new ones and the decline or even abolition of some old ones. Employees may resist a change because it affects their relative positions *vis-à-vis* other occupations, although in absolute terms they are no worse off.

Managers may be impatient with occupational resistance to change. They may feel that in a changing society the relative importance of different occupations is bound to change and that this is just something that people must adjust to. In particular, they may feel that if staff are protected from economic loss, they have no cause to complain; those who do are being unreasonable. In sum, they may be impatient – at such outmoded attitudes getting in the way of maximum productivity. But impatience is likely to do harm, especially if it makes them forget that much resistance to change is based on very solid reasons from the point of view of the affected individuals.

One of the most disturbing changes for individuals is that which reduces the value of their training and experience. This can happen when skill is replaced through mechanization or innovation, or when theoretical knowledge becomes more important than experience on the job. Employees may suffer economically through redundancy or lower earnings, or they may be economically protected but moved to a job that demands less skill and has a lower prestige. They may, particularly at the supervisory and managerial levels, remain in the same job but see their chances of promotion reduced by a change in the requirements for management jobs. Any change that reduces the value of employees' training and experience is likely to affect their sense of personal worth and their idea of their place in the company and in society. 'Tread softly because you tread on my dreams' might be amended, as a guide to those introducing change, to 'Tread softly because you tread on my sense of personal worth'. The prolonged coal strike in the UK in 1984 and early 1985 over the closure of uneconomic pits was but one, though a major, example of how strongly workers can feel about the loss of their way of life.

Resistance to change is often closely bound up with ideas of status. The status of people at any level may be threatened by change: the craftsman may become de-skilled; the manager who has come up the hard way may have lower prestige than the graduate manager. Change may threaten status in three ways: by redundancy and unemployment, by moving an individual to a position of lower status, and by lowering the status of a person's present job. The latter often happens in some mergers, where the distance from 'the boss' becomes greater. Managers who are used to reporting to the managing director may feel a considerable loss of status if they then have to report to an intermediary manager.

Employees may place a high value on their social relations in the neighbourhood and at work. Changes that affect these may be resisted. A change to a shift system will have a profound effect on life outside work and may be disliked in consequence. Social relations at work may be upset by changing the people with whom they are used to working, by altering the size of the working group or the relations with their boss.

Resistance to change will be intensified by fear. This will come from the realistic fears for security that employees who have invested the best years of their adult life in an organization are bound to feel. There may also be personal anxieties, which may not be fully conscious and are aroused by anything that can be interpreted as a threat. The latter, especially, may account for the fact that even changes that improve earnings and conditions may be viewed, at least initially, with suspicion and fear.

Helping adjustment to change

Change, especially rapid change, is often upsetting. Management must recognize this if it is to ease adjustment to change. Even in changes that will be beneficial from the employees' point of view there will be a period when they will have to expend more physical and emotional energy than usual in order to adjust to unfamiliar work or ways of working. Some research in America on perceived work pressure suggests that when this goes up, as it will during a change that means adapting to new methods of work, it affects workers' attitudes and leads to a drop in morale. At the least, change disturbs people's customary ways of doing things, which may make them fearful of what is going to happen to them. At the worst, it deprives them of their livelihood and destroys the value of their years of training and experience. Thus, change is often painful and may cause social casualties. It is likely to be resisted, especially if it affects people's livelihood, the value of their years of training and experience and their way of life. But there is now enough evidence from experience and research to show that the pains of change can be reduced and that resistance may be overcome or prevented if enough trouble is taken.

The human aspects of change need as careful planning as the engineering or financial. Planning should cover both the likely human effects of the change and what can be done to lessen those that are harmful. This may be done best by appointing a manager to be responsible for trying to reduce the human problems of change. Other managers are likely to be too busy to give these problems the attention needed. There are two aspects to managing change: planning and individual counselling. The planning should include a study of how a cut in the number of employees can, as far as possible, be achieved without compulsory redundancy, by provision for early retirement, careful plans for retraining that are adapted to the needs of different employees, protection against a drop in earnings during the retraining period, and help in getting another job. The timing and method of announcing the changes should also be well planned. Everything possible should be done to reduce the fear that comes from uncertainty and misapprehension. Such fear is likely to be the first effect of many changes. Giving clear information about how the cuts will be made and the options open to individuals, as well as individual counselling, can do much to allay fears and to help people understand and to assess what options are open to them.

Changes that affect the composition of working groups need special attention. Managers should never forget in their enthusiasm for planning the technical aspects of changes that many changes in the organization of work have effects on people. Many studies show that in designing the work organization more attention needs to be given to social factors if the best results are to be obtained in productivity and workers' satisfaction.

When management is planning changes in the organization of work, it should consider if it can do the following: increase the content of the job, provide more overlapping work within the individual work group, give the group greater responsibility, and encourage the supervisor to emphasize the technical and advisory aspect of the job. In sum, to give the individual groups greater responsibility for the work in which all can share, rather than each having a small self-contained job.

Research on changes in work organization shows that those who are likely to be affected by it should be told of what is planned and be consulted about what should be done, so that they have a say in how and when the changes that will affect them are introduced. The classic study of the value of involving workers in the process of change was carried out by Coch and French in a sewing factory employing about 600 people. The workers were paid by piece rates based on time study. In the past the firm had met strong resistance when it changed production schedules and methods; during the changeover periods production dropped, immediately and markedly, and frequently did not recover completely. There was also a high labour turnover and generally low morale. The experiment consisted of adopting a different method of introducing the change in each of three groups. The first group used the traditional method, in which top management issued an instruction to make the change and the workers and their immediate supervisors did not participate in the planning. The second group participated in the plan through representatives. In the third, all members participated. Production dropped initially in all groups, but much less in the third one. It also recovered much more rapidly in this group. The first, or non-participation, group showed no significant improvement of production during the first forty days after the changeover. During this time 17 per cent of the group left, compared with none in the other two groups. The first group also complained about the payment system and about individual managers, complaints which were not made by the other groups.[4]

Changes at any level can cause problems, not just those on the shop floor or in the office. The effects of rapid change on the organization of management can be far-reaching and, unless this is realized, it may result in inefficiency as well as frustration and strain. Rapid change increases the need for frequent personal contact between managers. Managers' jobs become more fluid, so that they cannot be set down in detailed job descriptions or prescribed by rules. The status that goes with the job may also become more indefinite. Managers will be judged at least in part by how they show up in the frequent discussions made necessary by change and under the pressure resulting from it.

Managers who fear uncertainty will feel insecure under the constant challenge of fluid rather than structured or prescribed relations. If the company is one where management rivalries are intense, rapid change may intensify them, as managers will no longer be able to retreat to their own defined jobs for protection – or if they seek to do so, as they may, so much the worse for the success of the change.

Rapid change can transform the nature of the manager's job, making it more fluid in responsibilities and in status. Successful managers will learn to live with, and to enjoy, the uncertainties that this will cause. They will be ready to search for the methods and the structure that are most suitable to the company's situation. When things go wrong, they will look for causes rather than finding scapegoats. Above all, they will see change as an exciting opportunity for cooperative and questioning endeavour.

Managing changes well is difficult but some clear lessons can be drawn from the results of research over the years. Do try to prevent unnecessary anxiety about what is going to happen. Do bring those likely to be affected by the change into the planning of what should be done. People are much more willing to accept, and to make work, something they help to create. Do not blame the troubles that arise on personal cussedness; they may contribute, but there are deeper causes. Do constantly re-examine what the organization is supposed to be doing and how it is doing it, with the aim of adopting whatever seem the most appropriate methods and structure. Do emphasize common tasks, both for the organization as a whole and for the individual groups, rather than separate jobs. Finally, do seek to encourage an atmosphere in which cooperative relations can flourish, rather than one in which people seek to score points or to assert prestige. The greater the change, the more important become human relations in determining its success or failure; hence the greater the need for the manager to understand human resistance to change.

Another important lesson is that change that requires a change in culture is difficult and takes time. A study of a major attempt to change the culture of the federal public service in Canada has lessons for similar attempts being made in many parts of the public sector in Britain. The conclusions of the Canadian study are:

1 Changing the culture of an organization is time-consuming and expensive and quite likely to fail.
2 It is much easier to change the culture of smaller organizations and where most of the employees are on the same site.
3 For a fundamental change, employees below senior management must have a strong perception of the need for change.
4 Major change in organizational values will lead to more staff turnover.[5]

Summary

Managers need to look outside their organization much more than they had to in the past. They must understand what aspects of their environment – political, economic, technical and social – both in their own country and abroad are likely to affect the problems they face. They must try to influence the environment where they can. They must learn to plan contingently and to adapt to the unforeseen.

Change, to be successful, must be carefully planned. Such planning must also include the likely human effects of the change and what can be done to ease adjustment to them. In such planning, managers can benefit from a knowledge of the most common causes of resistance to change. One of the greatest is fear. Much of it may be unnecessary and result from uncertainty and misapprehension. Some of it may be a reflection of the individual's unconscious fears triggered off by what is seen as a threat to security.

Resistance to change often comes from social barriers, of which the most important are the rigidities between occupations. Change may destroy a long-established relation between occupations. For the individual this can mean a loss in the value of training and experience, and with them a decline in status. Therefore, resistance to change is often bound up with the ideas of status.

There is sufficient evidence to show that much can be done to reduce resistance to change at all levels. Careful planning and consultation with staff, or their representatives, on details of the plan which affect them can do a great deal to enlist cooperation; the same is true for those who need to make changes at any level. People are likely to support what they help to create, but there are particular difficulties in trying to change the culture of an organization.

Part Four Managing Now and in the Future

11 Practical implications

This chapter summarizes for the manager the practical implications of the previous chapters. It offers help in identifying and coping with the most common problems of management. Such problems remain whatever changes take place. The end of the chapter reviews the ways in which the task of managing may change during the working lifetime of the reader.

Managing now: becoming a better manager

Managers' jobs differ greatly, but there are some common aspects to being an effective manager. The manager has to learn to manage himself or herself. Any manager who is in charge of other people has to learn how to get their commitment. All managers have to work with people other than their staff and have to learn the skills required to get their cooperation. Managers need to be thinking how to improve the efficiency of the operation for which they are responsible. This includes managing resources efficiently: particularly people, materials and equipment. Managers also need to be alert to the threats and opportunities that affect the unit for which they are responsible, whether it is a section, department, store, factory, hospital, school, charity, farm, prison or company. The nearer they are to the top of an organization, the more essential it is for them to think strategically about the future.

Managers who want to improve should review both their effectiveness and their efficiency. Effectiveness is doing the right things. Efficiency is making the most economical use of the resources. Effectiveness is more important than efficiency, because one must be doing the right kind of work. Only then does it matter whether the work is done efficiently.

Managing oneself

Learning to trust other people

This is one of the hardest lessons for new managers to learn: some never learn it. It is natural for many managers to find it difficult to trust others. They may have been promoted because they are more energetic and more efficient than the other people with whom they work. They may be correct in thinking that they would do a job better than their staff, but it may not be an effective use of their time to do so. Managing is getting things done through other people. A manager who thinks about what can be done only in terms of what he or she can do cannot be effective. Managing is not a solo activity, although some managers talk as if they depend solely upon themselves.

Managers must learn to accept their dependence upon other people. A key part of being a good manager is managing that dependence. Managers who say that they cannot delegate because they have poor staff may genuinely be unfortunate in the calibre of the staff that they have inherited or been given. More often this view is a criticism of themselves: a criticism either of their unwillingness to delegate when they could and should do so, or a criticism of their selection, training and development of their staff. The comment by Levinson is a useful warning – 'the successful executive is critical of his own performance; the unsuccessful of the performance of others'.[1]

Understanding one's own strengths and weaknesses

Such knowledge is an essential part of being a good manager – a knowledge that should improve as one grows older and hopefully becomes more mature. Managers need to understand their own strengths of character, outlook, knowledge and skills. They need, even more, to recognize their weaknesses and limitations. Weaknesses of character are perhaps more easily recognized than limitation of outlook. We all see the world through our own eyes, and what we notice and what we do not notice is distinctive. Self-knowledge can help one to assess what one can contribute and what is needed to complement the distinctive character of that contribution. Personality tests and assessment centres can help in this understanding. The Myers-Briggs personality test, based upon the theories of Jung, is a useful tool for managers who wish to understand how they perceive and judge the world, and which sides of their personality they have developed most.[2]

Two examples of how senior managers described what they thought to be their strengths and weaknesses may be helpful to readers in trying to review their own. The first manager described his strengths as follows: 'I rarely get irritated. I am single-minded so that if I see something that needs doing it will get done. I am technically competent. I have the ability to consult and to listen though I don't believe in committee decisions. I am practical: I always ask: "Will it work?"' He also said that he regarded his dogmatism as a strength because it meant that he was willing to say what he believed even if he was the only one to speak out. He thought that his main weakness was that he was a driver not a leader. He also lacked confidence, so that he started by thinking that others would do better than he would, though this did have the advantage of making him put in more effort.

The other manager saw her strengths as follows: 'I am highly stress resistant. I am responsive to new ideas. I am an extremely good decision-maker because I am willing to take decisions when they are, as most are, finely balanced, rather than to opt out by asking for more information. I get on well with people and am good at leading. I have a sense of humour and common sense.' This collection of very desirable managerial virtues was balanced by an awareness of weaknesses. She described her weaknesses as follows: 'I am not a natural delegator because I think that I can do it better and faster and am egotistical. I am too willing to sacrifice myself and others to the company. I don't suffer fools gladly and switch off too visibly if I am bored.' Weaknesses, she thought, were often the opposite of strengths – a remark that is a useful guide to understanding one's own weaknesses.

Coping with stress

An aspect of understanding oneself is being able to recognize one's own personal symptoms of stress. Each of us has our own warning signs that we have been pushing ourselves too hard. Indigestion, sleeping badly, irritability and excessive tiredness are common warning signs that should not be ignored. The danger is that the more overtired one gets, the more one may feel indispensable. Indeed, such a feeling is in itself a warning sign. Peter Nixon, when a consultant cardiologist at Charing Cross Hospital, produced a useful diagram of the relation between the amount of stimulus and the level of performance (Figure 11.1). The illustration shows that, for a time, being keyed up increases one's level of performance, but that there comes a point where this is more than one can take and one's performance begins to decline. If this is not recognized, people will continue to go downhill and be liable to a heart attack. The solution, Dr Nixon argues, is not drugs to suppress the symptoms but learning ways of backing off so as to reduce the extent to which one is keyed up. Managers need, if they are to continue to be effective under stressful conditions, to learn how to relax. When somebody is already fully stretched, relaxation will not be found in stressful pursuits like competitive sports. Such pastimes are for those who are still on the up-curve of the diagram.

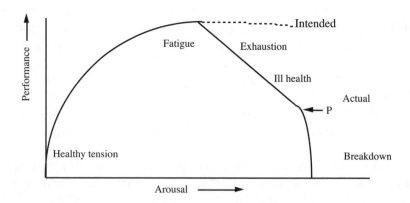

Figure 11.1 Nixon's Human Function Curve. (*Source:* Nixon, P. G. F., The Human Function Curve: with special reference to cardiovascular disorders, *Practitioner*, 1976, 217, 765, 935)

Many people are more prone to stress at some stages of their life than at others. The mid-life crisis is widely talked about as the main period of stress, but there are different cycles throughout life with periods of re-examination, anxiety and stress. Individuals who understand these stages can recognize what is happening and be better able to cope with them. A career should be seen in relation to stages in family life, particularly in two-career families, so that the couple do not subject themselves to too much pressure.

Self-development

Self-development is now recognized as an essential aspect of management development. Others may try to promote one's development through management education or a different kind of job, but whether one does develop depends upon oneself. There is a danger for all of us that as we grow older we become less able to adapt to change. There is another danger that we develop tunnel vision, so that our view of what can be done, and of possible solutions to problems, is too narrow. In some organizations this danger is recognized and training opportunities provided for all managers every year.

The best form of development is a challenging new job. Some organizations think about career development and aim to provide a succession of jobs that can encourage development. However, many managers are less fortunate: they may work for organizations that do not take management development seriously, or not be able to get a suitable job in another organization. Managers may then spend a long time in the same job, which can pose threats to development or even to the maintenance of one's performance. Figure 11.1 was about the desirability of an optimum amount of stimulus for performance. Where the job is not providing enough stimulus, one needs to search out other ways of remaining interested and alert or try hard to change one's job.

Many managers' jobs are very busy, so that managers must necessarily spend a lot of their time, and can too easily spend all their time, relying on the habits that they have developed. Self-development means trying to avoid being set in a mould of thinking and acting.

Effective use of time

Many managers would have put this first because it is the need that is most commonly recognized by those managers who wish to improve their effectiveness. It is not put first here because it is not the most important aspect of becoming a better manager. A good programme on the use of executive time can help managers to use their time more economically, but it cannot ensure that they are doing the right things. The distinction between the effective and the efficient use of time should be recognized. To improve the first, managers must decide what they personally ought to be doing. To improve the second, they can learn to organize their time better. Some people will find that one of the commercial time management systems helps them to do the latter. The utility of such systems depends upon the individual's temperament.

A very useful exercise for all managers is to keep a record of what they do in detail for a week or longer.[3] This can remove illusions about what one actually does. Many managers find that their picture of how they spend their time is different from what they really do. It is useful to check this out at intervals. A diary can help one to appraise the distribution of one's time between different aspects of the job and between different people. Both the content of what one is doing and the pattern of the day can be assessed. Was there, for example, any time during the week when one worked alone and uninterrupted for any useful period of time? If not, would it be desirable to make such time? Nobody can make time if they believe that they are indispensable, and must therefore be always available. Many managers have found that they can use their time better if they consider who they need to be available to and when. Regular meetings with staff are often a better use both of their time and of yours than an open-door policy. They can mean that you take time to discuss problems together, rather than just have frequent brief and fragmented interchanges.

Moral stamina

This is a different kind of heading from the previous ones, though it could be seen as an aspect of self-development. Because managing means working with other people, there are many opportunities for moral cowardice. The temptation to be liked and to be seen as a nice person may make the manager unwilling to talk frankly with staff or with colleagues. Managing other people necessarily means making judgements about them and at times taking difficult and sometimes painful decisions affecting them. A lesson that some managers have learned, sometimes too late, is that many people would prefer greater frankness about how they are doing and what are their career prospects than their boss thinks that they can accept.

Managers have a duty to help staff to develop their own moral stamina. Drucker put this well: 'A manager: Directs people or misdirects them; Brings out what is in them or stifle them; Strengthens their integrity or corrupts them; Trains them to stand upright and strong or deforms them.'[4]

Managing others

Managers necessarily work with and through other people, but who they have to work with and how difficult this is varies in different jobs.[5] The difficulty and importance of managing one's staff successfully varies considerably in different jobs. In some this is the main aspect of the job, in others relations with one's boss or bosses, with colleagues or with people outside the organization, may be much more important. The main problems in working successfully with other people are discussed below, though some will be much more important in some jobs than in others.

Enlisting commitment

The more common word is 'motivation': the phrase 'enlisting commitment' is used instead because it highlights what is needed. In Chapter 3 we traced the history of some panaceas that managers have thought would solve the problem for them. The history shows that there are no panaceas, but that what matters is the right attitude to people and an understanding of the dynamic between people and the way work is organized. This means accepting that most people want to do a good day's work but need a favourable setting in which to do it. Small groups and small establishments provide a better setting than large ones. People need to be involved if they are to be interested, and if they are to accept change. They need to be trusted if they are to behave responsibly.

Building and maintaining a team

A team can be defined as a group of people who pull together like a team of horses. The process of team-building is not easy. It requires the right mix of people, a task to which they can become committed, and one which is in the organization's interest. There are a number of different roles that need to be performed in a team if it is to work effectively. Hence, when recruiting a new person to a management group, one should think of what personal skills are missing to make the group more effective.[6]

Many managers who move companies often take some people with them. They may have chosen people who complement them and build up a new team whom they trust. They know that they will be more effective in their new job if they are supported by people who already form an effective managerial team. Good managers know that a group of people who have become a team will achieve far more than those who have not.

Living with touchiness

Employees are, and must be treated as, adults, but adults are touchy – some adults more so than others. Those who have remained married will have learnt what things upset their spouse and thus how to avoid some marital quarrels. Sensitivity to other people's feelings will help to avoid many otherwise unexpected problems. People vary in how they react, but yet there are some useful guidelines. Probably most important is that many people mind about their status, which should be recognized in making any changes. Managers should ask themselves 'In what ways could this change be seen as adversely affecting anyone's status?' Such preliminary thought can help to prevent difficulties later; some people are more status-conscious than others and are therefore more easily upset.

Trading successfully

Some managers will know at once what this heading means, but others may be perplexed. 'Trading' is one way of describing a balance of favours. For example, young couples in a housing estate may establish a baby-sitting group. It may be formalized so that a record is kept of who has sat for whom and how often, or it may be informal. Either way, some account will be taken of the exchange relationship. Many managers have to rely on colleagues in other departments or on people outside the organization if they are to get their work done. Such cooperation may depend at least in part upon the trading of favours. The formal organization can help to ensure the necessary cooperation but it is unlikely to make trading unnecessary. In some jobs it is easy – people want what you have to offer and are willing to give you what you need – but in others it is more difficult. You may be offering a service that is not widely accepted, you may want help that is costly for others to give. Managers who have to deal with people in other departments need to recognize where a trading relation exists and what they have to trade.

Trading relations exist both inside and outside the organization. The number of the latter are increasing as more services are being bought in from outside. Managers outside the purchasing department are likely to buy such services. As Leonard Sayles pointed out as long ago as 1964: 'Many employment relationships are being converted into contractual relationships: these require "trading" ability more than traditional "leadership".'[7] The trade is often not a purely financial one. Accountants and other service providers may be willing to work for you, and work for you well, for a variety of reasons other than pay. The reasons can be very varied. One may be the prestige of your organization: suppliers may be pleased to quote you as one of their customers. The interest of the work can be a major incentive for some service providers, particularly academics and computer consultants. The ambience of your organization and whether others enjoy working for you often matters, too. Good managers should know what are their trading counters with particular individuals.

Network-building

Increasingly managers require a wide range of contacts.
There are still jobs with a limited and specified set of people
with whom to work, but many jobs now require contacts
in other departments at different levels and with a variety of
people outside the organization. John Kotter, in his study of
15 general managers in the USA, was struck by the amount
of time that they spent establishing a network of cooperative
relations. This was a major activity during the first six months
in a new job. These networks often included hundreds, even
thousands, of individuals. Their typical network was so large
that he was unable to draw it in any detail.[8] Leonard Sayles
in his earlier study of engineering managers had found the
same thing, although on a smaller scale. Increasingly many
managers behave and need to behave like journalists in their
cultivation of contacts. This means getting to know a wide
range of people and keeping these contacts warm. The more
senior the manager, the more important is a good network
– 'good' meaning wide-ranging, friendly and informed in the
areas where the manager may need help. 'Help' can range
from finding another job to providing a service that is needed,
suggesting a good candidate for a vacancy, or knowing who
can help with a particular problem. Some managers are
natural network-builders. Others may need to learn the
importance of developing a supportive network.

Improvement projects

Good managers are not only trying to maintain the status
quo and cope with the problems and changes that come at
them, they are also trying to improve things. When one is
new in a job, it may be easy to see improvements that one
thinks need making – inefficiencies that one's predecessor
had not noticed or did not think were important – hence the
expression 'new broom'. When a manager has been in a job
for some time, it is easy to fall into a familiar pattern even
if it is mainly one of crisis-handling. Some managers who
have been in the same job for some time still keep alive their
belief that improvements are both possible and necessary.
One way of translating such a belief into action is to set

oneself improvement projects with objectives and measurable targets to a timescale. Some improvements can be effected in this formal way; others may have to be pursued more informally. Trying to change people's attitudes may mean looking for opportunities that will help to effect the change. A good manager both plans improvements and is on the alert for opportunities to promote change. A manager who thinks that no more improvements are possible, or necessary, should quickly try to find another job!

Managing the environment

This rather grand phrase applies to managers whose jobs and departments and companies are adversely affected by what is happening outside the organization. Nowadays more and more managers have contacts outside the organization; some of those who do not could and should have. 'Managing the environment' means that managers should not just be trying to react successfully to the adverse changes that come from outside the organization, they should be trying to prevent or moderate such changes. The organization's environment includes government, competitors, customers, suppliers of goods, services and people and the community. 'Government' for firms trading overseas means foreign as well as home government. Local government can be an important influence too.

Managers can often make the environment more favourable to themselves. This is true for many managers, not just those at the top. A simple example is cultivating the local schools so as to try to ensure a supply of good school-leavers. Another is getting to know relevant academics who may be able to help with a problem or interest a student in working on it. Cultivating politicians both at the national and local level is one way by which managers can try to get advance warning of changes that may be likely to affect them and try to influence what changes do take place. Taking care to be seen as a good neighbour by the local community can help to prevent trouble in the future. The aim should be establish a good reputation among the groups whose goodwill is important. Cultivating the relevant people is part of the network-building that many managers should be doing.

Managing in the future

No-one can know for certain what managing in the future will be like. We can be almost sure that there will be major unforeseen changes. Current changes provide some guide to the future. These changes are briefly discussed below.

Who has to be managed?

What it is like to manage is changing because the people to be managed have changed, and so has their relation to the manager. There is a continuing major shift in employment from manufacturing to service industries. Thus there are many fewer manual workers to be managed and far more people who are providing a service. Generally managers will be responsible for smaller groups of better educated staff.

Managers are now, and increasingly in the future will be, spending more of their time with people who are not their staff, and often may not be a fellow employee. Managing then becomes trying to enlist the cooperation of people in other departments or of suppliers or consultants outside the organization. These are trading relations rather than ones determined by the boss–staff hierarchy.

Anyway the boss–staff hierarchy has changed. Authority is, and is likely to continue to be, less acceptable than in the past. This reflects a major change in society: what has been termed the end of the grateful society. Better educated and more independent people expect to be consulted rather than to be told what to do.

A more recent change is the decline in the number of people employed in an organization because of subcontracting some services. This change seems likely to accelerate. Competitive pressure make the search for ways of improving efficiency more important. For some services, information technology also makes it much easier. Indeed, the term 'networking' has been coined for people who can work from home and be linked by computer terminal to the organization for which they are working. Such work may be paid for by a retainer or a fee rather than by a full-time salary; the former employee may also be expected to find other contractors.

What has to be managed?

Increasingly the answer is 'information' rather than physical resources: information about money, people and goods, information about targets and whether they are being met, information about possibilities and which are the most likely. Managers will increasingly have to know how to manage information in the sense of knowing what information they want and how to use what they receive. The danger is information overload making the manager's job harder.

Another answer is 'relationships'. This answer is implicit in the description of the changes in who has to be managed. Organizations, and hence managers, are much more exposed than in the past to a variety of interest groups. Managers have to try to establish good relations with those outside the organization whose goodwill can be important: national and local politicians, consumers, community groups and educationalists.

The managerial career

Short, fragmented and anxious might be the pessimist's prediction. 'Short', because the trend towards early retirement, at least from one's main employer, seems likely to continue. 'Fragmented', because more managers will have to change employers and may have spells of unemployment in between. 'Anxious', because of the greater insecurity and competitive pressures, improved performance monitoring and the stress from trying to cope with rapid change and an increased workload.

Challenging, fulfilling, varied and liberated might be the optimist's prediction. The first three because managers are likely to have more responsibility, greater variety, be called upon to manage a much wider range of people and to cope with more rapid change. 'Liberated', because they will not feel tied to one employer for life but will be able to change employers more easily, to start their own business or work on a fee basis from home. More managers will cease to be managers and take up other kinds of work.

References

Introduction to the Third Edition

1   Burgess, S. and Rees, H. (1996) Job Tenure in Britain 1975–92. *The Economic Journal*, 106, 435, pp. 334–344.
2   Bennis, W. (1995) The Essentials of Leadership. In *Mary Parker Follett: Prophet of Management* (P. Graham, ed.), p.178.

Chapter 1

1   Allen, R. E. (1990) *The Concise Oxford Dictionary of Current English*, 8th edn, Clarendon Press, Oxford.
2   Kast, F. E. and Rosenzweig, J. E. (1985) *Organization and Management: A Systems and Contingency Approach*, 4th edn, McGraw-Hill, New York, p.5.
3   French, D. and Saward, H. (1983) *Dictionary of Management*, 2nd edn, Gower, London.
4   Fayol, H. (1949) *General and Industrial Management*, Pitman, London. The date shows that it was a long time before his writings were widely available in English.
5   Carlson, S. (1951) *Executive Behaviour: A Study of the Work Load and the Working Methods of Managing Directors*, Strömbergs, Stockholm, p.24.
6   Mintzberg, H. (1973) *The Nature of Managerial Work*, Harper and Row, New York.
7   Drucker, P. (1955) *The Practice of Management*, Heinemann, London.
8   e.g. Drucker, P. (1989) *The New Realities*, Heinemann, London, although these ideas appeared in earlier books too.
9   Carlson, S. (1951) *Executive Behaviour*, op. cit.
10 Mintzberg, H. (1973) *The Nature of Managerial Work*, op. cit. A good summary of the research evidence available up to 1972 on managerial work in practice, as well as contributing an interesting and original analysis of the roles that managers have to play. A description of how 160 middle and senior managers in different organizations spent their time during four weeks is given in Stewart, R. (1988) *Managers and Their Jobs, A Study of the Similarities and Differences in the Ways Managers Spend Their Time*, 2nd edn, Macmillan, London.
11 Stewart, R. (1976) *Contrasts in Management: A Study of Different Types of Managers' Job: Their Demands and Choices*, McGraw-Hill (UK), Maidenhead, p.95.

12 Stewart, R., Barsoux, J. L. and Kieser, A. *et al.* (1994) *Managing in Britain and Germany.* Macmillan, London, p.92.

13 Sayles, L. R. (1964) *Managerial Behaviour: Administration in Complex Organizations*, McGraw-Hill, London, pp.140–141; and Prentice-Hall, Englewood Cliffs, NJ, 1982.

14 Stewart, R. (1976) *Contrasts in Management*, op. cit., Chapter 4.

15 Ibid., Chapter 2.

16 Kotter, J. (1982) *The General Managers.* The Free Press, New York.

17 Ibid., p.142.

18 Stewart, R. (1982) *Choices for the Manager*, McGraw-Hill (UK), Maidenhead, and Prentice-Hall, Englewood Cliffs, NJ.

Chapter 2

1 A wide coverage of the subject is given in Cooke, S. and Slack, N. (1991) *Making Management Decisions*, 2nd edn, Prentice-Hall International, Englewood Cliffs, NJ.

2 A useful practical book is Bazerman, M. (1993) *Judgment in Managerial Decision Making*, 3rd edn, Wiley, New York.

3 Cooke, S. and Slack, N. (1991) *Making Management Decisions*, op. cit., p.282.

4 An interesting example of this in deciding between three bridge alternatives for Los Angeles is given in Teasley III, C. E. (1994) Bridge over Troubled Waters: The Limits of Judgment in Decision Making. *Public Productivity and Management Review*, **XVII**, 4, pp.325–334.

5 Coopers & Lybrand/CBI (1994) *Survey of Benchmarking in the UK*, CBI, London.

6 Matheson, D., Matheson, J. E. and Menke, M. M. (1994) Making Excellent R&D Decisions. *Research Technology Management*, Nov–Dec., pp.21–24.

7 The study most often quoted is Pettigrew, A. M. (1973) *The Politics of Organizational Decision-making*, Tavistock, London. A more recent study of 150 decision in 30 very varied organizations is Hickson, D., Butler R. J. and Cray, D. *et al.* (1986) *Top Decisions: Strategic Decision Making in Organizations*, Basil Blackwell, Oxford.

8 Morris, P. W. G. and Haugh, G. H. (1987) *The Anatomy of Major Projects: A Study of the Reality of Project Management.* Wiley, New York.

9 Gore, W. (1960) in a paper for the Acton Society Trust's annual conference.

10 Neustadt, R. E. and May, E. R. (1986) *Thinking in Time: The Uses of History for Decision Makers*, The Free Press, New York, p.37.

11 Rodrigues, S. B. and Hickson, D. J. (1995) Success in Decision Making: Different Organizations, Differing Reasons for Success. *Journal of Management Studies*, **32**, 5, pp.655–678.

12 Ibid., p.655.

13 Martin, N. (1956) Differential Decisions in the Management of an Industrial Plant. *Journal of Business*, **24**, 4, pp.249–260.

14 Mintzberg, H., Raisinghani, D. and Theoret, A. (1976) The Structure of 'Unstructured' Decision Processes. *Administrative Science Quarterly*, **21**, 2, p.274.

Chapter 3

1   Burns, T. (1954) Directions of Activity and Communications in Departmental Executive Group, *Human Relations*, **VII**, 1, p.95.

2   Rabinowitz, W., Falkenbach, K., Travers, J. R., Valentine, G. and Weener, P. (1983) Worker Motivation: Unsolved Problem or Untapped Resource? *California Management Review* **XXV**, 2, pp.45–56.

3   Tillsley, C. (1994) Employee Involvement: Employees' Views. *Great Britain – Dept. of Employment – Employment Gazette*, **102**, 6, pp.211–216.

4   Wanguri, D. M. (1995) A Review, an Integration, and a Critique of Cross-disciplinary Research on Performance Appraisals, Evaluations, and Feedback: 1980–1990. *Journal of Business Communication*, **32**, 3, pp.267–293.

5   For example, the effective opposition of British employers to the industrial charter proposed by those who first set up the Federation of British Industries, which would have guaranteed minimum wages, granted generous redundancy payments, and provided fringe benefits.

6   Tillsley, C. (1994) Employment Involvement: Employees' Views, op. cit.

7   Kessler, I. and Undy, R. (1996) *The New Employment Relationship: Examining the Psychological Contract*, Issues in People Management, No. 12, Institute of Personnel and Development, London.

8   Locke, E. A., Schweiger, D. M. and Latham, G. P. (1988) Participation in Decision Making: When Should It Be Used? In *Participative Management. Organizational Dynamics Special Reports*, American Management Association, pp.1–15.

9   Narasimhan, P. S. (1950) 'Profit-sharing: A Review'. *International Labour Review*, Dec, pp.469–499.

10 Ibid., p.481.

11 Finance Act 1978 (Chapter 42), Part III, Chapter III, HMSO, London.

12 British Institute of Management (1978) *Employee Financial Participation*, BIM, London.
13 *Financial Times* (1984) Aug. 1. The figure of 7,000 cannot be compared with the 1978 survey as that was of a limited number of companies.
14 Casey, B., Lakey, J. and White, M. (1992) *Payment Systems: A Look at Current Practice*, Policy Studies Institute, Department of Employment, London, p.34.
15 Information about quality circles is taken from Bradley, K. and Hill, S. (1983) After Japan: The Quality Circle Transplant and Productive Efficiency. *British Journal of Industrial Relations*, Nov., pp.291–311.
16 Ibid., pp.307–308.
17 Davidson, G. (1995) Quality Circles Didn't Die – They Just Keep Improving. *CMA Magazine*, **69**, 1, p.6.
18 Geary, J. F. (1994) Task Participation: Employees' Participation Enabled or Constrained? In *Personnel Management: A Comprehensive Guide to Theory and Practice in Britain* (K. Sisson, ed.), p. 640.
19 Jacob, R. (1993) TQM: More Than a Dying Fad. *Fortune*, Oct. 18, pp.66–72.
20 Troy, K. and Schein, L. (1993) Creating a Service Quality Culture. In *The Service Quality Handbook* (W. F. Christopher, ed.), Amacom, pp. 111–123.
21 Grant, R. M., Shani, R. and Krishnan, R. (1994) TQM's Challenge to Management Theory and Practice. *Sloan Management Review*, **35**, 2, p.25.
22 Miller, W. H. (1995) The Future? Not Yet. *Industry Week*, **244**, 8, Apr. 17, p.73.
23 Marriott, R. (1971) *Incentive Payment Systems: A Review of Research and Opinion*, 4th edn, Staples Press, London, p.94.
24 Income Data Services Study No. 140 (1977) *Income Pay Schemes* **I**, Feb.
25 Eilon, S. (1992) *Management Practice and Mispractice*, Routledge, London, p.167
26 Ibid., p.166.
27 Guest, D. (1984) What's New in Motivation? *Personnel Management*, May, 20–3.
28 McGregor, D. (1960) *The Human Side of Enterprise*, McGraw-Hill, New York.
29 Blackburn, R.M and Mann, M. (1979) *The Working Class in the Labour Market*, Macmillan, London.
30 Peters, T. J. and Waterman, R. H., Jr. (1982) *In Search of Excellence: Lessons from America's Best-Run Companies*, Harper and Row, New York.

31 McGregor, D. (1950) Changing Patterns in Human Relations, *Conference Board Management Record*, **12**, 9, p.366.
32 Ouchi, W. G. (1981) *Theory Z: How American Business Can Meet the Japanese Challenge*, Addison-Wesley, Boston.
33 Guest, D. (1984) What's New in Motivation? op. cit., p.22.

Chapter 4
1   For brief biographical accounts and comparisons, Gardner, H. (1995) *Leading Minds: An Anatomy of Leadership*. HarperCollins, London; for lessons from a leader, Harvey-Jones, J. (1988) *Making it Happen: Reflections on Leadership*, Collins, London; for a helpful analysis, Bennis, W. and Nanus, B. (1985) *Leaders: Five Strategies for Taking Charge*, Harper and Row, London. For a more specific, practical approach, Stewart, R. (1995) *Leading in the NHS: A Practical Guide*, 2nd. edn, Macmillan, London.
2   *Collins Concise Dictionary* (1995) revised 3rd edn, Collins, London.
3   Bass, B. M. (1990) *Bass and Stogdill's Handbook of Leadership: Theory, Research, and Managerial Applications*, 3rd edn, The Free Press/Macmillan, New York.
4   Edwards, R. S. and Townsend, H. (1965) *Business Enterprise: Its Growth and Organization*, Macmillan, London. p.33.
5   Argyris, C. (1953) *The Personnel Journal*, **32**, 2, pp.50–55.
6   Cox, C. J. and Cooper, C. L. (1988) *High Flyers: An Anatomy of Managerial Success*, Basil Blackwell, Oxford, pp.157–162.
7   Bass, B. M. (1990) *Bass & Stogdill's Handbook of Leadership*, 3rd edn, op. cit., p.87.
8   Shartle, C. L. (1957) *Executive Performance and Leadership*, Staples Press, London, pp.120–122.
9   Halpin, A. W. (1954) The Leadership Behaviour and Combat Performance of Airplane Commanders. *Journal of Abnormal and Social Psychology*, **XLIX**,1, pp.19–22.
10 Blake, R. R. and Mouton, J. S.(1994), *The Managerial Grid*, Gulf, The first edition was published in 1964 and the third in 1985.
11 Ibid., p.324.
12 Ibid., pp.325–327.
13 Management Centre Europe (1988) Leadership: The Attitudes and Opinions of European Managers. Excerpt in Syrett, M. and Hogg, C. (1992) *Frontiers of Leadership: An Essential Reader*, Blackwell, Oxford, p.239.
14 Yukl, G. (1994) *Leadership in Organizations*, 3rd edn, Prentice-Hall, Englewood Cliffs, NJ.
15 White, M. and Trevor, M. (1983) *Under Japanese Management: The Experience of British Workers*, Policy Studies Institute, Heinemann, London.

16 Belbin, R. M. (1993) *Team Roles at Work*, Butterworth-Heinemann, Oxford. This is a later version of his earlier work which was published in 1981, *Management Teams: Why They Succeed or Fail*, Heinemann, London.

17 Tannenbaum, R. and Schmidt, W. H. (1958) How to Choose a Leadership Pattern. *Harvard Business Review*, **36**, 2, pp.95–101. This classic article is reprinted in different collections of readings, including Koontz, H. and O'Donnell, C. (1976) *Management: A Book of Readings*, 4th edn, McGraw-Hill, New York.

18 Bronn, P. S. and Lorange, P. (1996) Management Education, Future Of. In *International Encyclopedia of Business and Management*, Vol. 3 (M. Warner, ed.), Routledge, London, p.2724.

19 Khandwalla, P. N. (1996) Management Education in India. In *Internationational Encyclopedia of Business and Management*, Vol. 3 (M. Warner, ed.), ibid., p.2803.

20 Tichy, N. M. (1996) GE's Crotonville: A Staging Ground for Corporate Revolution. In *How Organizations Learn* (K. Starkey, ed.), pp.243–257.

21 Ibid., p.248.

22 Miller, E. L. (1996) Management Education and Development, International. In *International Encyclopedia of Business and Management*, Vol. 3 (M. Warner, ed.), op. cit., p.2747.

23 Whyte, W. H. (1956) *The Organization Man*, Simon and Schuster, also Jonathan Cape, London, 1957.

Chapter 5

1 Weber, M. (1964) *The Theory of Social and Economic Organization*, first English translation by Henderson, A. M. and Parsons, T., The Free Press of Glencoe, New York.

2 Heckscher, C. and Donnellon, A., eds (1994) *The Post-bureaucratic Organization: New Perspectives on Organizational Change*, Sage, London, pp.1–2.

3 Nohria, N. and Berkley, J. D. (1994) The Virtual Organization: Bureaucracy, Technology, and the Implosion of Control. In *The Post-bureaucratic Organization: New Perspectives on Organizational Change* (C. Heckscher and A. Donnellon, eds) ibid., p.111.

4 Benveniste, G. (1987) *Professionalizing the Organization: Reducing Bureaucracy to Enhance Effectiveness*, Jossey-Bass, p.260.

Chapter 6

1 Stewart, R. (1993) *The Reality of Organizations*, 3rd edn, Macmillan, London.

2   PA Consulting Group (1996) *1996 International Strategic Sourcing Study*, PA Consulting Group, London.

3   Peters, T. J. and Waterman, R. H., Jr. (1982) *In Search of Excellence: Lessons from America's Best-Run Companies*, Harper and Row, New York.

4   Conference Board (1995) *HR Executive Review: Redefining the Middle Manager*, Vol. 2, Conference Board, p.2.

5   Haire, M., ed. (1959) *Modern Organization Theory: A Symposium of the Foundation for Research on Human Behaviour.* John Wiley, New York and Chapman and Hall, London, p.2.

6   Urwick, L. (1952) *Notes on the Theory of Organization* American Management Association,

7   Woodward, J. (1958) Management and Technology. *Problems of Progress in Industry*, No. 3, Department of Scientific and Industrial Research, HMSO, London, p.37.

8   Croome, H. (1960) Human Problems of Innovation, based on a study by Burns, T. and Stalker, G. M. No. 5, Department of Scientific and Industrial Research, HMSO, London, p.12.

9   Lawrence, P. R. and Lorsch, J. W. (1967) *Organization and Environment, Managing Differentiation and Integration*, Harvard University, Division of Research, Graduate School of Business Administration, Cambridge, Mass.

10 Simon, H. A. Guetzhow, H., Kozmetsky, G. and Tyndall , G. (1954) *Centralization v. Decentralization in Organizing the Controller's Department*, Controllership Foundation Inc. Reissued 1978, Scholars Book, Accounting Classic Series, Houston, Texas.

11 Ibid., p.5.

12 Pugh, D. S. and Hickson, D. J. (1989) *Writers on Organizations*, 4th edn. Sage, London, Chapter 1.

13 Mintzberg, H. (1983) *Structures in Fives: Designing Effective Organizations.* Prentice-Hall, Englewood Cliffs, NJ.

14 Butler, R. J. (1991) *Designing Organizations: A Comparative Approach*, Routledge, London.

Chapter 7

1   Barnard, C. (1958) *The Functions of the Executive.* Harvard University Press, Cambridge, Mass., p.225 (originally published 1938, Oxford University Press).

2   Barnard, C. (1958) *The Functions of the Executive*, ibid., p.226.

3   Turner, R. H. (1947) The Navy Disbursing Officer as a Bureaucrat. *American Sociological Review* **12**, pp.342–348.

4   Ibid., pp.347–348.

5   Hopper, T. M. (1980) Role Conflicts of Management Accountants and Their Position Within Organization Structures. *Accounting, Organizations and Society*, **5**, 4, p.408.

6   Walker, C. R. and Guest, R. H. (1952) *The Foreman on the Assembly Line*, Harvard University Press, Cambridge, Mass.
7   Trist, E. L. and Bamforth, K. W. (1951) Some Social and Psychological Consequences of the Longwall Method of Coal-Getting. *Human Relations*, **4**, 1, pp.3–38.
8   Emery, F. E. and Trist, E. L. (1960) Socio-Technical Systems. *Management Sciences: Models and Techniques*, Vol. 11, Pergamon Press, Oxford, p.81.
9   Hackman, J. R. and Oldham, G. R. (1980) *Work Redesign*, Addison Wesley, Boston, pp.77–88.
10 Fried, Y., Cummings, A. and Oldham, G. R. (1996) Job design. In *International Encyclopedia of Business and Management*, Vol. 3 (M. Warner, ed.), Routledge, London, p.2424.
11 Cotton, J. L. (1993) *Employee Involvement: Methods for Improving Performance and Work Attitudes*, Sage, London.
12 Gallie, D. and White, M. (1993) *Employee Commitment and the Skills Revolution: First Finds from the Employment in Britain Survey*, Policy Studies Institute, Heinemann, London, Chapter 6.
13 Moore, W. (1996) All Stressed Up and Nowhere to Go. *The Health Service Journal*, **106**, p.5519, Sept. 5, pp. 21–25.
14 Vinten, G. (1996) Whistleblowing. In *International Encyclopedia of Business and Management*, op. cit., Vol. 5, p.5031.
15 Beach, L. R. (1993) *Making the Right Decision: Organizational Culture, Vision, and Planning*. Prentice-Hall, Englewood Cliffs, NJ.

Chapter 8
1   President Coolidge in a message to the nation, 1924.
2   Stewart, R., Barsoux, J. and Kieser, A. *et al.* (1994) *Managing in Britain and Germany*, Macmillan, London; Ebster-Grosz, D. and Pugh, D. (1996) *Anglo-German Business Collaboration: Pitfalls and Potentials*, Macmillan Business, London, pp.210–211, 219.
3   Barsoux, J. and Lawrence, P. (1990) *Management in France*, Cassell, London.
4   Weinshall, T. E., ed. (1990) *Culture and Management*. Quoted in Lawrence, P. (1996) Management in Europe. In *International Encyclopedia of Business and Management*, Vol. 3 (M. Warner, ed.), Routledge, London, p.2846.
5   For a general description of the reports of these teams, see Hutton, G. (1953) *We Too Can Prosper: The Promise of Productivity*, Allen and Unwin, London.
6   Anglo-American Productivity Council (1949) Internal Combustion Engines, *Productivity Team Report* Anglo-American Productivity Council, p.7.

7   Heavy Electrical EDC, Report of the Study Group visit to North America (1984) *New Technology: Manpower Aspects of the Management of Change*, National Economic Development Office, London, p.2.

8   Lorenz, A. and Smith, D. (1993) Secret Report Reveals Shocking State of Industry. *The Sunday Times*, 14 March, p.l.

9   White, M. and Trevor, M. (1983) *Under Japanese Management: The Experience of British Workers*, Policy Studies Institute, Heinemann, London, p.138.

10 Ibid., p.139.

11 Stewart, R. *et al.* (1994) *Managing in Britain and Germany*, op. cit.

12 The Acton Trust Society (1956) *Management Succession.* The Trust, London, p.8.

13 Stewart, R. and Duncan-Jones, P. (1956) Educational Background and Career History of British Managers, with some American Comparisons. *Explorations in Entrepreneurial History*, **IX**, 2, pp. 61–71.

14 Poole, M., Mansfield, R., Blyton, P. and Frost, P. (1981) *Managers in Focus: The British Manager in the Early 1980s*, Gower, London, p.42.

15 'Social distance' is the term used by sociologists to describe the extent to which individuals or groups willingly consent to share certain experiences. The smaller the social distance, the more willing they are to share intimate experiences. Sociologists have measured the amount of social distance between different groups by asking people whether they would admit a particular group to lose kinship by marriage, to being neighbours in the same street, etc.

16 Croome, H. M. and Hammond, R. J. (1947) *An Economic History of Britain*, revised edition, Christophers, London, pp.159–160,

17 Fox, A. (1966) *Industrial Sociology and Industrial Relations*, Research Paper 3, Royal Commission on Trade Unions and Employers' Associations, HMSO, London.

18 Purcell, J. and Sisson, K. (1983) Strategies and Practice in the Management of Industrial Relations. In *Industrial Relations in Britain*, (G. S. Bain, ed.), Blackwell, Oxford.

19 Ibid., p.114.

20 Ibid., p.115.

21 Gallie, D. (1978) *In Search of the New Working Class: Automation and Social Integration within the Capitalist Enterprise*, Cambridge University Press, Cambridge.

22 Ibid., p.296.

23 Sweeney, K. (1996) Membership of trade unions in 1994: an analysis based on information from the Certification Officer. *Labour Market Trends*, **104**, 2, p.49.

Chapter 9
1   Edwards, R. S. and Townsend, H. (1965) *Business Enterprise: Its Growth and Organization*, Macmillan, London, p.183.
2   Daniel, W. W. and Millward, N. (1983) *Workplace Industrial Relations in Britain*, The DE/PSI/SSRC Survey, Heinemann, London, p.218.
3   From a speech to General Motors' sales committee, 29 July 1925, quoted by the Temporary National Economic Committee (1941) *Relative Efficiency of Large, Medium-Sized and Small Business*, Monograph 13, US Government Printing Office, Washington, pp.130–131,
4   Mueller, D. C. (1992) Mergers. In *The New Palgrave Dictionary of Money and Finance* (P. Newman, M. Milgate and J. Eatwell, eds.), Macmillan, London.
5   Meeks, G. (1996) Acquisitions and Divestments. In *International Encyclopedia of Business and Management*, Vol. 1, Routledge, London, pp.154–162.
6   Hannah, L. (1976) *The Rise of the Corporate Economy*, Methuen, London, p.216.
7   Edwards, R. S. and Townsend, H. (1965) *Business Enterprise: Its Growth and Organization*, op. cit., p.195.
8   Schumacher, E. F. (1974) *Small is Beautiful*, Abacus, London, p.202.

Chapter 10
1   Drucker, P. F. (1969) *The Age of Discontinuity*, Heinemann, London, p.248.
2   Drucker, P. F. (1973) *People and Performance: The Best of Peter Drucker on Management*, Heinemann, London, p.24.
3   See also Stewart, R. (1991) *Managing Today and Tomorrow*. Macmillan, London, Chapter 8 where there is a wider discussion of the managerial implications of IT.
4   Coch, L. and French, J. R. P. (1948) Overcoming Resistance to Change. In *Human Relations*, Vol. I, Tavistock Publications, London, pp.512–532.
5   deCarufel, A. (1994) Organizational Culture Change for Public Sector Managers. *Optimum*, **25**, 2, pp.16–24.

Chapter 11
1   Levinson, H. (1968) *The Exceptional Executive*, Harvard University Press, Cambridge, Mass., p.254.
2   Myers, I. B. (1962) *The Myers-Briggs Type Indicator*, Consulting Psychologists Press, Palo Alto, Cal.
3   Stewart, R. (1988) *Managers and Their Jobs, a Study of the Similarities and Differences in the Ways Managers Spend Their*

Time, 2nd. edn, Chapter 8, 'Lessons for the Manager' provides some examples.

4   Drucker, P. *People and Performances: The Best of Peter Drucker on Management*, Heinemann, London, p.55.

5   These differences are discussed in Stewart, R. (1976) *Contrasts in Management: A Study of Different Types of Managers' Jobs: Their Demand and Choices*, McGraw-Hill (UK), Maidenhead.

6   Belbin, R. M. (1993) *Team Roles at Work*, Butterworth-Heinemann, Oxford, gives a useful account of the different roles that people may play in a team.

7   Sayles, L. (1964) *Managerial Behaviour: Administration in Complex Organizations*, McGraw-Hill, New York, p.65.

8   Kotter, J. (1982) *The General Managers*, The Free Press, New York, p.67.

Index